I0110467

To know and not to do is not to know.

Wang Yang Ming

Copyrights © 2025

All Rights Reserved

No part of this book may be reproduced or transmitted in
any form or by any means, electronic or mechanical,
including photocopying, recording, or by any information
storage and retrieval system without the written permission
of the authors, except where permitted by law.

Why did we write this book?

WHAT CAN WE DO BY FRIDAY? is a call to think differently. To act.

It is a prompt to start small and accelerate.

Not to wait for the stars to align or the bottom line to always make sense.

Why? Because acting against climate change is not another chapter of our history.

It is THE transformation of the 21st century, requiring us to change the way we think, move, eat, and live. Once we all agree on the nature of this transformation, we can think differently about our own individual role.

WHAT CAN WE DO BY FRIDAY? is not a book to critique and dismiss because there is still uncertainty. It's a book to use as a field guide for action, *because* there still is uncertainty.

Above all, it's a call to start NOW.

Onwards,

David & Tony

Meet the Authors

David Benattar

David Benattar is a global sustainability leader and adviser.

Over the last seven years, David spearheaded the sustainability transformation at The Warehouse Group, New Zealand's largest publicly listed retail group. David was a member of New Zealand ministerial delegation at COP25 in Madrid and COP26 in Glasgow.

David began his career at Aveda, a Minneapolis-based pioneer in natural beauty, before joining the Earth Pledge Foundation in New York, where he pioneered early-stage sustainability solutions in the construction, apparel, food and waste sectors, and contributed to public policy during the Bloomberg administration.

David has collaborated with global sustainability organisations, including NRDC, WWF, WRI, and WBCSD. He has advised clients including DuPont, Kering, L'Oréal, LVMH, Mitsubishi, PwC, United Technologies, and others

David holds an executive MBA from Oxford University, Saïd Business School, where he is exploring the application of Artificial Intelligence to climate transition planning.

David, a French national, is a runner and an exhibited street photographer. See www.benattar.photography

Tony Balfour

As a globally experienced senior executive in a wide range of industries and categories, with a strong track record of success leading innovation and market/category development, Tony has worked with some of the world's best brands.

He has been a director on the Boards of Silver Fern Farms, Methven Industries, Mt Difficulty Wines, The Warehouse Group, Les Mills International, and Blis Technologies, and Bluelab.

He is currently on the Board of RealNZ tourism, Agnition Ventures (agtech) and Pioneer Energy (renewable energy) and Chairs Ecogas – New Zealand's first waste to energy biogas operation.

He sits on a number of advisory boards and mentors emerging leaders.

Tony recently self-published *A Word in Your Ear, a Field Guide for Virgin Directors*, where he shares insights that change professional directors' approaches to their jobs. See www.tonybalfour.com

The greatest threat to our planet is the belief that someone else will save it.

Robert Swan

In loving memory of

gardener

sailor

architect

builder

&

sustainability pioneer

Leslie Hoffman

In memory of American labor mediator Theodore W. Kheel, who early on understood the need to solve the conflict between environmental preservation and economic development.

May their teachings prevail.

Contents.

We think of climate change as slow, but it is unnervingly fast.

We think of the technological change necessary to avert it as fast arriving, but unfortunately it is deceptively slow.

Especially judged by just how soon we need it.

David Wallace-Wells,

The Uninhabitable Earth: Life After Warming

Foreword

God calling.

Sustainability is religion. Here is how I entered its church.

I arrived in New York in 1995. Hypnotized by the City's jazz I moved there from my native France to pursue a career in the cosmetics industry. It had just the right amount of glam for the aspiring marketing executive I was.

After countless rejections, I was hired by Aveda, a small yet mighty hair care brand and one of the first to treat nature as the holy spirit. Aveda philosophy was "the art of pure plant flowers and plant essences". What it meant was beauty products free from silicone, parabens, synthetic fragrances, mineral oil, and other nasties widely found in other mass-market brands at that time.

Aveda was encouraging its customers to eat its Uruku lipstick, made with pigments grown by the Yawanawa tribe in the Amazon Forest. Why? Because women ingest a good portion of their lipsticks, and traditional mineral oil rich lipsticks with synthetic ingredients derived from petrochemicals are not as tasteful as they look. Aveda knew its product formulas and consumer marketing well. The brand went on to be acquired by The Estée Lauder Companies and became one of the most successful and profitable beauty brands in the industry. Nature sells.

After four years of hands-on education, I was looking for a new challenge. I joined the Earth Pledge Foundation, a non-profit steered by environmentalist Leslie Hoffman and chaired by legendary mediator Ted Kheel. Both had phenomenal grit and an address book counting the who's who of American business and politics. From 2001 to 2005, they had me work on the early stage of the corporate sustainability movement. We developed Anaerobic Digestion to manage New York City's organic waste, promoted city-wide implementation of vegetated rooftops to reduce energy consumption, and created one of the first sustainable fashion initiatives, collaborating with the likes of Armani, Marc Jacobs, and Stella McCartney. Life in New York felt grand. Mike Bloomberg, who at that time was running New York with a tight grip, engaged us to help him shape what a modern city should look like: green, healthy and prosperous. That was just before the Enron scandal, the 2008 Global Financial Crisis, and the BP Deepwater Horizon oil spill.

Green was replaced by greed. I moved on to a new role.

Move forward to today, December 2024. COP27 just closed. I spent the past seven years of my life embedding sustainability in New Zealand's largest retail group, The Warehouse Group, a mass market operator with a global supply chain and a mission to "help New Zealanders live better every day". One step at a time, The Warehouse Group sourced all its stores' electricity from solar farms, updated its products packaging and ingredients with more sustainable options, organised electronic and plastic waste recycling in its stores, and became carbon neutral in its operations. We developed countless other initiatives to embed climate action in every step of our business activities. The Warehouse Group's founder, its CEO, board of directors, and team members lived with the core belief that green was good for business and that Sustainable & Affordable was the right thing to do for our customers.

"How do you eat an elephant?" an old man asked. One bite at a time, he advised. This incremental approach guided our work at The Warehouse Group.

It was early on in my life at The Warehouse Group that I met Tony Balfour, a defining Kiwi bloke with a mountainous profile, an adept of sharp words who cut close to the bone, a company director, an expeditious pundit, a practitioner of Essentialism, a world-class executive, and an advisor turned friend. Tony lives by the Da Vinci principle that simplicity is the ultimate sophistication. When I mentioned writing a book on climate action, Tony jumped in. The shape and form you will read here are the product of our dialogues.

Through this book, we've wanted to turn our experiences into snippets of intelligence - windows of quick advice to inspire readers to take action.

While there is a great deal of money already available to decarbonise of our economy, the industry is missing hands-on agents of change. People focused on finding new solutions and implementing the ones already available now. People designing the new business, operating, and financial models that the world needs to meet our climate and sustainability goals. There is nothing fancy about it. It's all urgent. You've seen the numbers but let me mention one unfortunate newsflash.

2024 is slated to be the warmest calendar year on record going back to 1850, surpassing all previous records. Average global temperatures have exceeded 1.5°C above pre-industrial levels for the first time. Extreme weather has swept across the globe: severe drought hit Italy and South America, fatal floods devastated Nepal, Sudan and Spain; heatwaves in Mexico, Mali and Saudi Arabia killed thousands, and multiple disastrous cyclones hit the U.S. and the Philippines.

The burning of fossil fuel that powers the global economy continues to increase atmospheric concentrations of carbon dioxide and methane. In 2023, carbon emissions increased by 30% compared to 2022, driven largely by persistent wildfires in Canada. The list goes on.

So yes, we invite you to read this book in any order. We invite you to share it with others, to start conversations, and provoke new ways of thinking. But more importantly, we prefer you put this book down and spend your time doing more of the actions that will turn this ship around. Or sway it to a better place – the place that ensures future generations will live comfortably, as they should. as we did.

Without further ado. Go do.

David

10 Numbers We Need to Change.

1. The carbon footprint of individuals
2. The levels of air pollution in key cities worldwide
3. The percentage on fossil fuels in the global energy mix
4. The share of electric vehicles on the road
5. The amount of fossil fuel burned by airlines
6. The quantity of plastic waste discarded into landfills
7. The amount of microplastic we ingest daily
8. The chemical fertilizers dumped into soil and aquifers
9. The methane emissions from livestock
10. The percentage of companies with credible climate action plans

What Can You Do by Friday?

Move into action.

5 little facts.

Little fact 1

Climate change is a mega bomb. It breaks all systems.

Wildfires, hurricanes, and floods are causing economic mayhem, migrations, conflicts, and suffering.

It's unfolding here and now in front of us.

Climate change means more than extreme weather. It's about water scarcity, ocean acidification, ecosystem erosion, biodiversity collapse and numerous other interconnected forces that are hard to grasp.

Little fact 2

Climate change mechanics are both simple and complex.

The burning of fossil fuel, the old engine of industrialisation - has disrupted the earth's digestive system.

As we pump more CO_2 into the atmosphere than nature can absorb, the concentration of carbon particles in the atmosphere increases. This creates a heat trap that changes the dynamics of weather patterns.

That is the complicated, intractable, and yet somewhat simple issue we're not addressing at the required speed.

If we stop emitting emissions now, if we turn off the faucet of carbon emissions, if we shift our energy sources and transform industry, the pattern will reverse.

Little fact 3

Climate change is costing all of us a ton of cash. But most of us don't see it.

It increases our cost of doing business, our insurance premiums, the price of food and healthcare, infrastructure repair and maintenance, and in fact everything close or distant to the making of our economic backbone.

Consider this example: Your cousin Gregoire manages a ski resort in the French Alps. Ski seasons are shortening. Depending on how fast we take action, scientists predict that only around 30% of French ski resorts will be able to help maintain a 100- day ski season by 2050 (*Peeters, 2023*).

What will Gregoire do? He can indeed go run an artificial snow indoor ski resort in Dubai. But something is telling us he will lose his *joie de vivre*.

There are millions of Cousins Gregoire in every sector of activity. There are potato farmers in Idaho and construction workers in California who are seeing their working conditions deteriorate because of the impact of climate change

And there are the trillions of dollars required to transition every segment of our global economy to the green economy.

All of it is expensive, urgent, and feasible.

Little fact 4

Climate change is easy to see and yet hard to grasp.

Its impact is material but also incredibly abstract.

How do we experience sea level rise? How do we connect a rainier summer to climate change?

We don't. Scientists do.

It makes the coordination of people, finance, and politics incredibly hard.

Why? Because most differ in opinions on how we should address this long-lived disease we can't touch and feel.

Little fact 5

Despite the headwinds, we are making progress.

Probably because, as Martin Luther King Jr said, the arch of history bends toward justice.

But also, thanks to people like you.

You, engineers, scientists, journalists, politicians, investors, teachers, farmers, architects, lawyers, advertising executives, or community leaders.

You, every single one of you, taking small or big steps to address the effects or the causes of climate change around you.

What can you do by Friday?

Read this book and give a copy to your boss.

Section 1:

Mindset & Motivation

A letter to my Unborn Granddaughter.

4th April 2024

Open on: April 4th, 2050

Dearest Emma,

I will be a photo on the bookshelf by the time you read this. I want you to know I tried.

I drove my electric car, and I recycled my plastic. But it wasn't enough.

I grew a few vegetables, and I bought a jacket from the Salvation Army.

But it wasn't enough.

I complained about the coal companies, and I stopped buying bottled water from France.

But it wasn't enough.

I promised to reduce my company's emissions by 75% by 2050.

But it wasn't enough.

I did my bit. It wasn't enough. And I knew it all along.

I am so sorry.

Granddad

The Climate Wager: Betting on Our Planet.

In 1670, Blaise Pascal, the legendary French mathematician, envisioned a thought experiment that 350 years later is still provocative – the Pascal Wager.

Picture a simple coin toss.

Heads – you win: daily bliss in paradise for all of eternity.

Tails – you lose: the minor inconvenience of a daily prayer and a Sunday church sermon.

In Pascal's Wager the potential reward – eternal happiness – dwarfs any earthly sacrifice.

The bet? Believing in God.

The logic? Even if God is a figment, you don't lose that much.

But if he exists, jackpot!

In 1670 it was considered blasphemous under the threat of death to even hypothesise the absence of God. But with Pascal's clever wager, even early devil-worshipping atheists might have had pause for thought. What's the harm?

In 2024, swap God for Earth. And faith for action.

Imagine an investment opportunity with staggering odds.

Heads – we win: safeguarding the only home we've ever known and securing a thriving future for generations to come. Tails – we lose: a few more salads, an EV, and a holiday at the local beach instead of Fiji.

Welcome to the Climate Wager.

So, which side of the Climate Wager will you choose? Heads, for a liveable future or tails, for an uncertain roll of the dice?

Forget divine rewards. Here, the stakes are tangible and immediate. We stand at a crossroads, facing the devastating consequences of inaction on climate change. Every delayed transition, every unnecessary emission, increases the risk of losing a liveable planet.

The good news? Taking personal action, no matter how small, alters the odds. Switching to clean energy, embracing sustainable practices, and advocating for change – these are our "bets" on a future worth inhabiting. The potential gain? An Earth bathed in vibrant ecosystems, thriving communities, and a legacy of responsible stewardship.

Sure, there are inconveniences. But consider the price of inaction: extreme weather events, extinctions, and dwindling resources – a grim reality that dwarfs any temporary discomfort.

This isn't just about moral obligation; it's about a strategic wager on our collective future. Every individual shift ripples outwards, inspiring others, influencing policies, and accelerating the transition towards a sustainable future.

What's the worst that could happen if you take action?

What can you do by Friday?

Place your first bet. Pick the most "obvious" sustainable switch you've been thinking about – You know it's the right thing to do probably but you just haven't got round to it. Flip a coin. Heads: you make the change right now. Tails: you still make the change, because that's the point of the chapter. No more weighing odds that are already in our favour.

Never doubt that a small group of thoughtful, committed citizens can change the world; indeed, it's the only thing that ever has.

Margaret Mead

Fuck the Planet. Save Yourself.

The planet is going to be fine.

No, really, the planet is going to be fine.

It's been here before. It thrived through asteroids; ice ages; volcano eruptions; pandemics; World Wars and Michael Bublé Christmas concerts. It will come out the other side and do something amazing. Life will go on as miraculously as ever.

Just this time without humans.

And a few thousand other species.

This is not about altruism or doing good, it is about being deeply selfish - saving ourselves.

You can be as altruistic as you like, or you can be selfish. It doesn't matter. The action will be the same. Save yourself and your future family.

Why?

Because it's your family.

What Can We Do by Friday?

See the chapter title

It's about Life and Death.

Last time I spoke at a business conference, an innocent soul asked: "why should business leaders attend the COP summits?".

COP summits, for those of you who don't know, are the yearly United Nations summits tasked with instructing the world economy and its leaders to act in a sensible way. In a way that science is telling us will maintain life on earth as we know it today, where the global temperature increase will stay within 1.5 degrees against the pre-industrial age.

I snapped: "because it's about life and death".

As we progressed through the conference, speakers gave various diplomatic reviews of the political process and business justifications for participating in Cop conferences, whether they take place in Paris, Madrid, Glasgow, Sharm El Sheik, Dubai, Azerbaijan, and soon in Belém, Brazil.

At the end of the conference, someone else commented, "David was probably exaggerating when he said it's about life and death, but I do believe that COP conferences are where business leaders go to learn about climate change, speak about their transition plans, and make deals". It was a polite audience.

The moderator asked for closing remarks.

I snapped again. "Business leaders attending COP conferences, business leaders taking climate action, is about Life and Death.

Those who don't understand and yet are asleep at the wheel. It's about staying relevant in a world that is increasingly defined by the climate actions we take. And it's about life and death for our physical ability to sustain ourselves on our planet as we know it today."

What can we do by Friday?

Sit in the boardroom, grab the microphone, and state the obvious. Your friends and colleagues will thank you for it.

I Love My Wife.

I *think* this to myself all the time.

And I *tell* her occasionally.

I *do* it rarely.

It might look something like this:

Think Think Think Think Think Think Talk Talk Talk Talk Talk Talk Talk Talk Talk Talk Talk Talk Think Think Think Talk Talk Talk Talk Talk Talk Think Think Think Talk Talk Talk. Do. Talk Talk Talk Talk Talk Talk. Do. Talk Talk Talk Talk Talk Talk Talk Talk Talk Talk Talk. Do. Talk Talk Talk.

Love is a verb - a *doing* word.

So is sustainability.

One tiny act is vastly more important than any big sentence.

If I want to really love Sarah it needs to look more like this.

Do Do Do. Talk. Do Do Do Do Do Do Do Do Do. Talk. Think. Do Do Do Do Do Do Do Do Do Do Do Do Do Do Do. Think. Do Do Do Do Do Do . Talk. Do Do Do Do Do Do Do Do Do Do Do .

If talk and PowerPoint solved climate change, it would have been done in 2006.

What can you do by Friday?

Pick the one sustainability commitment you talk about most often. Now do it three times without telling anyone. No social media posts, no explaining why, no discussing your plans. Just three quiet acts of doing.

Have a plan.

A list. Do it. Start again. Do it. Start again.

Long journeys start with one step.

One job at a time – done.

Do what you can with what you have.

Norwegians call it the doorstep mile.

No journey starts until you take the first step.

Mars: Anyone?

You may have missed it - the little dot in the middle of the page, a few inches above. If you stood on Mars and looked back at Earth it would be the size of that dot. Well, almost.

What you need to do is rip this page out of the book and pin it on the wall.

Then walk 17.3 metres away from the wall. For most of us that is about 20 or 21 strides.

Now look at the dot.

That is Earth viewed from Mars.

All of it. You and me. Our 8,000,000,000 neighbours. The Elephants. The Ants. The Oceans. The whales. Your children. Taylor Swift. Lionel Messi. Elvis. Your dog, Luca. All on that dot you cannot see.

We are not relocating to Mars anytime soon.

What can you do by Friday?

Find a quiet moment to recreate this Mars perspective experiment with someone you care about.

Mark a dot on a piece of paper, measure out those 17.3 metres together, and stand there in silence for one full minute. Then talk about how that makes you feel about our shared home.

500.

You find it hard to measure time passing by. 280

Your granddaughter Emma. Just yesterday. She was a sweetheart of an angel. 360.

You used to hold her hand in your palm, manoeuvring her through her first stumbling steps. 365

Her teenage years. Moving past the verge of innocence. 370

One evening she comes back home, barely holding tears. 375

Her first love crush. 380

You still see her as your angel. 385

Look back. 390

It's not only Emma whose years passed by you. 400

It's also the tragedy playing around her. 410

Emma cannot regain her innocence. 420

The increase in carbon parts per million in the atmosphere can. 423

What can you do by Friday?

Join the millions working passionately to turn around the carbon destiny of the world economy.

Why?

So that Emma doesn't live in a world where 500 follows a full stop.

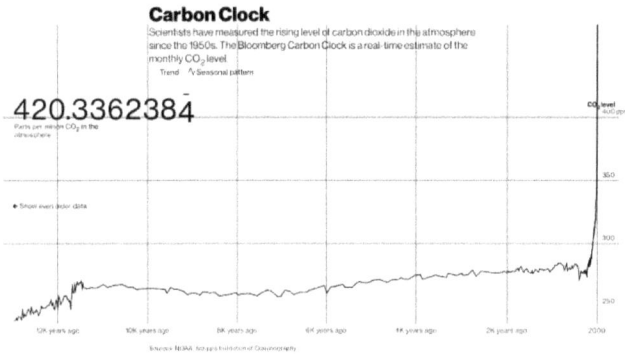

Carbon Clock

Scientists have measured the rising level of carbon dioxide in the atmosphere since the 1950s. The Bloomberg Carbon Clock is a real-time estimate of the monthly CO_2 level.

Trend /\ Seasonal pattern

420.3362384

Parts per million CO_2 in the atmosphere

• Smoothed older data

CO_2 level 400 ppm

350

300

250

12K years ago   10K years ago   8K years ago   6K years ago   4K years ago   2K years ago   2000

Sources: NOAA, Scripps Institute of Oceanography

The CO_2 level in the atmosphere could be compared to the world's thermostat.

As of January 2025, CO2 makes up about 426 parts per million (ppm) of our air. Before the industrial age, around 1860, the concentration of carbon dioxide (CO_2) in the atmosphere was approximately 280 parts per million.

CO_2 levels increased since we began the burning of fossil fuels, deforestation, and industrial processes.

The greatest obstacle to living is expectancy, which hangs upon tomorrow and loses today. The whole future lies in uncertainty. Live immediately.

- Seneca

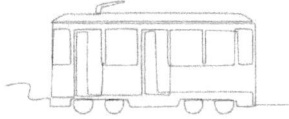

Look Away Now?

You probably know the trolley problem - introduced by philosopher Philippa Foot in her 1967 paper "Abortion and the Doctrine of Double Effect."

It relates to choice-making when the "right" option is not obvious.

There have been many derivations of the problem. The original scenario proposed by Foot is this:

A trolley (tram) is heading towards five people who are tied to a track and cannot move. You are standing next to a lever that can divert the trolley onto another track, where there is one person tied up.

Do you pull the lever?

Sacrificing one to save five, or do nothing and let the trolley kill the original five people?

You can be a bystander and let fate take its course.

Or you can act and reduce the destruction. But not without cost.

Seems obvious: you choose the lesser evil and kill one.

You probably know where I'm going here.

The world is facing a global scale trolley problem.

Do you look away and let the trolley maintain its relentless course?

Or do you help pull the lever, even though you know there will still be pain. Maybe for you. And if you delay, tomorrow it might be 10 people, or 100, or 1,000,000.

What can you do by Friday?

Choose one significant climate impact you've been avoiding thinking about - perhaps your flight habits, meat consumption, or fast fashion purchases. Instead of planning or contemplating, take one irreversible action right now. Cancel a flight, clear out your fast fashion apps, or call your pension provider about their fossil fuel investments. No more postponing the pull of the lever.

The greatest danger to our future is apathy. We can't all save the world in a dramatic way, but we can each make our small difference, and together those small differences add up. Every single person makes an impact on the planet every single day. The question is: What kind of impact do you want to make?

Jane Goodall

The Billion-Dollar Dilemma.

Let's pretend:

After a demanding work week, you decide to take a relaxing walk.

Suddenly, you notice something unusual.

An odd protuberance sticks out of the ground.

You bend down, and scratch at it.

Your fingernails come out greasy.

You bend down again, scratch further, and your fingers turn dark and oily.

Let me break the news.

You've just stumbled upon oil reserves.

Right there, in your backyard.

You've found an oil well.

And let's pretend there's coal right next to it.

You've hit the jackpot.

You have $20 billion worth of fossil fuel reserves buried beneath your garden, quantities enough to worsen climate change.

What do you do next?

Option 1: Keep quiet. Don't tell anyone. Never say a word to your wife or children. Don't go buy that house in the south of France, a mansion for your aging parents, or the Ferrari you've always dreamt of.

Option 2: You want to cause no harm, but truth is, you need a bit of cash. So you go to the World Bank and strike a deal where you commit to never burning the fossil fuels in exchange for a reduced payment. You may not get the $20 billion or the Ferrari, but you could still buy your wife a diamond and your aging parents a cottage.

Option 3: You sell the oil to the highest bidder, guaranteeing you'll be rich forever. Your granddaughter may live in a world of more extreme weather conditions, but she'll get a good umbrella and be all right.

Now, imagine you're an ordinary person barely getting by. How do you make such a monumental decision?

Let's shift reality again.

You are now the leader of a struggling nation with one of the world's worst health indices and lowest average lifespan.

What do you decide to do?

How should global institutions - the World Bank, the IMF, and the UN - support you in making decisions about burning fossil fuels when the country you lead face such dramatic socio-economic challenges?

How could you resist the temptation to achieve the prosperity others have gained by burning coal, oil, and gas?

What can you do by Friday?

Global institutions, banks, insurers, and private investors can collaborate to create a compelling business case for acting *now* instead of delaying action and paying a higher price later.

Why? because today we can calculate with reasonable accuracy the future cost of pollution and more extreme weather events on our health, communities, and economies.

In short, we can invest today to secure a brighter future for all tomorrow.

This is not an advertising tagline.

The Age of Innocence.

The age of innocence is over.

And so is the age of abundance.

As French president Emmanuel Macron declared in August 2022, "What we are currently living through is a kind of major tipping point or a great upheaval … we are living the end of what could have seemed an era of abundance … the end of the abundance of products, of technologies that seemed always available … the end of the abundance of land and materials, including water."

Our modern society, the outcome of the industrial revolution amplified by globalism and consumerism, led to a linear extractive economy built on abundant and affordable natural resources.

This game is over.

How do we change that?

By integrating sustainable methods in everything we do.

By advocating for what brings us closer to a new bright modern economy, one that balances out economic growth with conservation and climate action.

By upgrading our methods of extraction, production, transportation and consumption.

By addressing the cost benefit of our choices.

By embracing the unknown, and the possibilities that a thoughtful, enlightened future can bring.

What can you do by Friday?

We are not innocent bystanders.

One decision at a time, each decision moves us in the right direction.

Or not.

Anyone who thinks you can have infinite growth on a finite planet is either a madman or an economist.

Kenneth Boulding

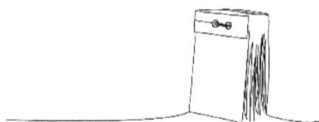

It's Tomorrow.

We do not need to panic - nor do we need procrastination.

We need clear-headed urgency.

As the Nike advertisement says:

"Yesterday You Said Tomorrow."

Well - it's tomorrow.

Section 2:

You as a Consumer.

The Marshmallow Test.

In 1969 Walter Michelle, a professor at Stanford University, began what would become one of the most famous psychological studies ever undertaken.

'Cognitive and Attentional Mechanisms in Delay of Gratification' was published in 1972 in the 'Journal of Personality and Social Psychology.'

In the complex world of science, it was a remarkably simple test, and it used a humble household confectionery.

You probably know it as the "The Marshmallow Test".

The experiment was designed to study delayed gratification—the ability to put off instant rewards for better outcomes in the future.

Young children were tempted with a single marshmallow on a plate placed right in front of them. They were left in the room alone for 15 minutes.

If they gave in to temptation, they got to eat that one marshmallow.

If they resisted the temptation, they were rewarded with two marshmallows at the end of the 15 minutes.

On average one-third of the young children resisted the temptation of the immediate reward (one marshmallow) to receive a greater reward later (two marshmallows).

It is one of the most reliably replicated experiments into human nature ever conducted.

The most important finding, and one that is often overlooked, was that resistance to temptation as a young child correlated strongly with better outcomes later in life. In areas such as academic success, health, relationships, and general well-being – outcomes were statistically significantly above average for the young "resistors".

Imagine you're that kid in 1969, sitting in a room with a marshmallow in front of you. Do you eat it now, or wait and get two? No brainer, right?

But here's the twist: what if the marshmallow is not a fluffy treat, but it's the only planet we call home?

Welcome to the Adult version of the marshmallow test, AKA: the climate crisis.

Today is our marshmallow test.

For all eight billion of us.

Will we continue to give into the temptation right in front of us. The convenience. The pleasure. The conventional solutions.

Or can we resist.

Eating the marshmallow now might mean no marshmallows for anyone in the future.

How do we apply the lessons from those Stanford preschoolers to our current predicament?

First, understand that waiting for that second marshmallow – or, in our case, investing in sustainable practices – isn't about willpower - it's about trust. Trust in the promise of a better future, trust in our leaders to make the right decisions, and trust in each other to resist today's marshmallow.

Secondly, it's about knowledge.

Just as children who understood the value of waiting for the second marshmallow were more likely to succeed - educating people, mainly yourself, about the long-term benefits of environmental conservation can make it easier to make sustainable choices.

And thirdly, we need to make the wait for that second marshmallow as tempting as possible.

What can you do by Friday?

Identify a "marshmallow" in your life - something convenient but unsustainable that you regularly consume or do. For just this week, resist it. Write down how it feels each time you say no. By Friday, reflect: was the resistance as hard as you imagined? What was your "second marshmallow" - the benefit you gained or noticed from waiting?

Every man is guilty of all the good
he did not do.

Voltaire

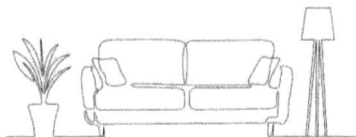

I Need a New Couch.

If you are amongst the privileged classes – and let's face it, anyone reading this book is – you are also most likely suffering from the Diderot Effect.

An invasive illness that is exhausting the planet's resources.

Here's how it works.

You buy a new couch. Now your rug looks shabby, so you buy a new rug. Now your coffee table doesn't quite go, so you get a nice replica Noguchi, and that demands a couple of never to be read coffee table books to finish it off. Which reminds you to get that library shelves installed. So you buy 73 books to make it look just-so.

They are all nice, but none were necessary.

That's the Diderot Effect – a spiralling cycle of consumption.

Named after the French philosopher Denis Diderot, it's the modern addiction to continually upgrading your possessions. An addiction that did not emerge until the 1960s.

How much spiralling?

It's estimated that over our lifecycle, the average western household will purchase enough household goods to furnish between 7-10 houses (and that does not include necessary technology upgrades).

And that's just part of it. Businesses do the same. Only worse.

The simplest path to sustainability, without actually *doing* anything, is love what you have. Not what you don't.

Just stop.

What can you do by Friday?

Start a spreadsheet and capture a list of the things you wanted to buy - but didn't. See how quickly it adds up. Take pride in it.

The Invisible Hand.

Since 1990, more than 1 billion people have been lifted out of extreme poverty worldwide.

In the same period, the number of deaths attributable to air pollution could be upwards of 200 million.

Two sides of the same coin called Capitalism.

Can we rewire it?

The redistribution of biological wealth in the soil of forests is an ecological prowess. Mycelium acts both as nutrients and a communications network, an invisible web that redistributes nutrients equally and ensures that no tree is left behind.

Life carries on symbiotically and magnificently.

Adam Smith's invisible hand is its economic equivalent. It acts as an imaginary market force redistributing economic outcomes for the wellbeing of all.

Yet, the invisible hand allows for 200 million air pollution victims. And countless other ailments.

The invisible hand needs a better brain. A better software. A better something that takes us where we want to be, in a symbiotic magnificent forest.

Which tools should we use to take us there?

Plenty of them:

1. Carbon data. Carbon tax. Carbon markets.
2. Carbon Capture. Carbon sequestration. Reforestation.
3. Blue Carbon. Regeneration. Adaptation.
4. Nature as a service.
5. Green and clean tech.
6. Artificial Intelligence.
7. Wind, Solar, Biomass, and nuclear.
8. Smart grid, satellite imagery, eco-mobility.
9. Bio materials, recycling, circularity.
10. Sustainable finance, impact investment, philanthropy.

We use today's tools, reprogram the brain, and get a better hand.

We create new governance, financial systems, and education. We do not ignore our mistakes, and we study our masters.

What can you do by Friday?

Put this book down. Pick your tool. One or several of them. Apply them to yourself, your business, or your community.

Start a meeting with a mantra. Meditate. Do.

Check the numbers. Join the movement. Make progress against the world's largest problems.

Stop Looking for the $600 Seat Post.

In the early 2000s I was caught under Lance Armstrong's spell and like millions of people around the world took up road cycling.

Of course, I had to have a Trek bike like the ones the US Postal team were riding, so I splashed out.

I was at SBR (Swim Bike Run) a high-end bike store in Melbourne having it fitted (I didn't know you had to have bikes fitted but it was a very worthwhile exercise) when I became aware of seat posts.

A seat post is the tube that connects your bike saddle to the bike's frame. It looks like an offcut of pipe you might see lying around in a plumber's yard.

I had never thought about that part of a bike, until I saw somebody come into SBR and spend $600 on one. Remember, this was 2002 – you could fly across the Pacific for $600.

Why $600? Because it was Titanium. 120 grams lighter than a standard seat post.

The shop owner, Bevan, told me he sold two or three a month. Then he dropped this gem:

"The funny thing is, if the rider just lost 120 grams of weight themselves, it would have the same effect. And it would be free."

There it is.

The allure of the easy tech fix. The silver bullet. The new putter. The new oven. The new protein powder.

Sound familiar? It should. We do this with climate change *all* the time.

We wait for the perfect electric car while our gas-guzzler idles in the driveway. We hope for fusion power while leaving lights on in empty rooms. We dream of carbon capture technology while buying our 12th summer dress.

We're all hoping for our $600 seat post to turn up.

Climate change doesn't need a titanium solution. It just needs us to lose some weight. The world doesn't need one person doing sustainability perfectly. It needs millions doing it imperfectly.

It's not as sexy as a shiny new gadget. It's not as easy as swiping a credit card. But it's materially more effective.

Turn off a light. That's a few grams. Walk to the store. There's a few more. Choose chicken over beef. Add a salad. Another few grams.

Small actions. Repeated daily. That's how real change happens.

The $600 seat post might make you feel like you're doing something. But it's the everyday decisions that move the needle.

What $600 seat post are you waiting for? What future solution are you procrastinating over?

You don't need $600 of titanium. You just need to start pedalling.

What can you do by Friday?

Go through your sustainability wish list - those expensive eco-gadgets or perfect solutions you've been waiting for.

Pick three basic, no-cost actions you could do instead.

Cross off one big-ticket item from your list and replace it with these three simple habits.

Start them today, not someday. They might not be titanium-plated, but they'll get you moving.

It is not the strongest species that survives, nor the most intelligent, but the one most responsive to change.

Charles Darwin

Dinner Table Decisions.

There are many decisions you can make around the dinner table that you can't make around the board table.

Here are six that shape your household's carbon footprint:

> How you heat your home
>
> How you heat your water
>
> How you commute
>
> How you cook
>
> When (or if) to install solar panels
>
> When (or if) to install solar batteries

These choices are the backbone of your personal environmental footprint. They are not trivial.

Why? Because they are "set & forget" decisions.

Unlike daily recycling or occasional air travel, these are one-time choices with lifetime impact. That makes them especially powerful.

They are some of the easiest gains you can make.

Think of them as investments. In your home. And in your planet. Make the right call once, and the benefits last your lifetime.

Take your car, for instance. If it is not an EV, it's your home's biggest carbon culprit. And your spouse's car. And your daughter's car.

Sometime in the next few years you will change your car. That's a one-off opportunity to slash your emissions.

Switching to an electric vehicle isn't just a purchase. It's a choice. A commitment to a cleaner future that ripples through your daily life. If you have the finances, it is hypocritical to drive an internal combustion car and (claim to) be committed to sustainability.

The same goes for your home's heating system, water heater, and cooking appliances. Each change is a chance to lock in a lifetime of sustainability.

Solar panels and batteries? They're not just about saving money. They're about energy independence and reducing grid strain.

These decisions might feel daunting. You don't have to make all these changes at once – indeed the timing is almost certain to be spread out. Just start with what's next. Whether it's your car, your heating, your oven.

Maybe it's switching to an induction cooktop or installing a smart thermostat.

Each choice shifts your mindset. Suddenly, you're not just a consumer. You're an active participant in shaping a sustainable world.

And it all starts at your dinner table. With conversations about the future you want to create.

These aren't just household decisions. They are legacy decisions. They help shape the world your children will inherit.

What can you do by Friday?

So next time you sit down for a meal, consider: What's your next sustainability move? How can your home become a vote for change?

Your dinner table isn't just for eating. It's where you can change your world, one decision at a time

Section 3.

You in your Community.

Don't be a Parrot.

Too many people let others decide what they like, what they feel, who they support, what they believe.

Outsource your water problems to your plumber.

Outsource your car problems to a mechanic.

Outsource your cooking problems to McDonalds if you must.

But don't outsource your thinking.

Especially not to a 7-word headline on today's Instagram list.

Especially when it comes to something as important as climate change.

Do not be a parrot. Stand for something.

It is too easy to sleepily adopt the opinions of the people: your professor, your downstairs neighbour, your hairdresser, or your favourite TikToker.

Outsourced thinking becomes homogeneous, change-resistant, and numbingly simplified. Just because it looks good on the front of A T shirt doesn't mean it's right.

Once you outsource your thinking on big issues, you are halfway down the road to outsourcing your life.

What can you do by Friday?

Inform yourself.

I am only one, but still I am one. I cannot do everything, but still I can do something; and just because I cannot do everything, I will not refuse to do the something that I can do.

Helen Keller

94% of All Humans are Dead. And Soon You Will Be Joining Them.

Tick fucking tock. Your time is running out.

The question is: What will you do?

Climate change isn't just another issue. It's *the* issue. The one that will define our era. One way or the other.

"What did they do when they knew?" Will be the topic of a million school essays in 100 years' time.

Because we do know.

The science is clear.

The clock is ticking.

But here's the thing about clocks: They don't care about your excuses. They don't wait for convenient moments. They keep fucking ticking.

Next week, becomes next month, becomes next year.

And then, you're dead. And some years later, no one will care that you ever existed.

Climate action isn't a spectator sport. It's a game you play. A life and death game.

Even if you don't pick up the ball, you are still on the field.

You can plant a forest in your mind. Or grab a shovel and plant one tree.

You can sunbath in Bali. Or put solar panels on your roof.

Dream of clean oceans. Or recycle your trash.

Snowballs get bigger. But only if you start one

Those 94% of humans are dead: They are not doing anything about climate change.

You're alive. You have power. You have a choice.

What can you do by Friday?

Tick fucking tock.

Nuts.

There is a very grainy video on YouTube that is over 20 years old and has been viewed (collectively in all its versions) well over 100 million times.

It's called: First Follower - Leadership Lessons from Dancing Guy. Take a look.

It's just 2 minutes 57 seconds long. But in that short time it tells a powerful story about building community and momentum.

Its message is not about leadership. It's about followship.

It's set at an undetermined music festival where one shirtless, awkward man (who may be under the influence of something) starts dancing alone as if no one is watching. In the middle of a vast, passive, crowd.

Even though the dancing man occupies the screen for the entire video, he is not the hero. The hero is the first follower. The person who gets up and dances alongside the dancing man.

Sometimes it requires more courage to be the first follower than the original lone innovator. Almost always.

Because the lone innovator has belief and a degree of self confidence, potentially delusion, while the first follower has to drop their own ambition and scepticism and go all in on the innovator's vision.

It's a powerful thought when it comes to sustainability.

Watch what happens in that video: It takes a long time for the first follower to join in, but once he does, a third person stands up. Then a fourth. Within less than a minute, what started as one "crazy" dancer becomes a crowd of dozens, all moving to the same beat.

Soon, anyone not dancing looks like the odd one out.

This is how movements work. Almost always.

They don't start with grand speeches or perfect plans or everyone jumping to their feet immediately. They start with one person doing something different, and then— and this is the crucial part—another person is brave enough to say "That thing you're doing? I believe in it too."

In the climate movement, we already have our dancing heroes. The scientists who've been sounding the alarm for decades. The innovators experimenting with wild ideas that might just work. The first brave soul to bike to work when it's raining. The first family in the neighbourhood to put solar panels on their roof.

But here's what trips us up: Our first inclination is to critique their dance moves, instead of joining the dance.

Maybe the mushroom farmer growing carbon-negative building materials isn't perfect, yet. Maybe the person turning old fishing nets into skateboards can't solve the entire ocean plastic crisis. Maybe the neighbourhood tool library seems small and inefficient compared to Amazon.

But they're all dancing. Toward something better.

Being a first follower means supporting these imperfect pioneers. It means seeing past the early clumsy moves to recognize the bigger rhythm they're creating. It means understanding that movements don't need perfection—they need participation.

First followers transform the lone nut into a leader.

They show others it's safe to join in. They turn a moment into a movement by saying "The direction matters more than the dance steps."

So when the lone nut in your network starts composting at the office, or experiments with a cargo bike for deliveries, or launches a repair café in their garage—don't wait for others to validate it first. Don't hold back until they've perfected their moves.

Stand up.

Join in.

Start dancing.

What can you do by Friday?

Find the "weird" sustainability practice that you've been secretly admiring but were too self-conscious to try. Maybe it's bringing your own containers to the bulk store or starting a lunch leftovers club. Do it publicly by Friday - not perfectly, just visibly. Then invite a friend to join you. And next week get that person to invite a friend.

Ripple Affects.

Yes, I know it should be Effects.

In this case, it's not. It's Affects.

Not the outcome, the process.

In a world consumed by fact-free rants and tribalism, small genuine acts become especially powerful.

Your pebble, thrown in the right pond, can catalyse an endless ripple of positive change.

You might feel your gestures are insignificant, but tiny personal acts possess a remarkable ability to sow the seed of change.

"Showing up" is powerful.

Our life's path is carved by what we show up for. And the things we don't show up for.

The difference between showing up and not – that *is* your life.

Small acts, more than big words, bring people together.

Rosa Parks not moving seats. Colin Kaepernick taking the knee. Greta Thunberg. Whina Cooper. Harvey Milk. Tank Man. None of them set out to change the world.

But they did. They showed up.

Not by comment or criticism. By deeds. They committed.

First with the small pebble.

And then other people joined in with their pebbles too.

What can you do by Friday?

Choose one climate action you've been nervous about doing in front of others - cycling to work, bringing containers to the deli, using the library. Do it proudly, publicly, and repeatedly. Not to preach, just to be seen doing it. Your pebble isn't just about the splash - it's about being spotted throwing it.

Pessimists Write the Headlines. Optimists Write the Future.

It's an interesting quirk of nature that pessimists can easily sound wise and thoughtful by predicting fire and brimstone, while optimists can sound like snake oil salesmen predicting sunshine and joy.

Pessimists make the news while optimists rarely do.

If you don't believe me go and read the top 10 headlines of your news platform de jour. Unless there is a story about the incumbent leader of the country praising his own efforts before re-election, my bet is that all 10 stories will have a negative slant.

If it bleeds it leads is both cliched and sadly true. It's not just bad news - it's a *pessimistic* slant on bad news.

Mercifully, following Newton's Third Law of Motion (it's the one about equal and opposite force) while the pessimists mutter and shuffle their worry beads, it's the optimists who get on with the work.

There is a lot to be pessimistic about. Once you are pessimistic you are only one stop away from being fatalistic, which is only one stop away from giving up.

Optimists don't give up. Optimists don't believe in serendipity. They believe there is a solution and they will set about finding it. Famously Thomas Edison failed over 5000 times to create a working light globe. For a pessimist that would have been more than enough evidence to suggest it couldn't be done. For Edison, it was another reason to say he was one step closer to the solution.

I mean it comes to climate change 5000 attempts may be just a start. We may need millions of attempts. The good news is there are millions of people making those attempts. You can choose to be one of them or not.

There are several reasons to be optimistic:

Optimists get it done. While pessimists wring their hands.

Optimists create the future. Pessimists critique the status quo.

Optimists lift others. Pessimists drag others down.

Optimists create friends. Pessimists create accomplices.

Optimists empower. Pessimists entrench.

Optimists vote. Pessimists complain.

What can you do by Friday?

Life is a choice.

The best time to plant a tree was 20 years ago. The second best time is today.

Chinese proverb

Future Possible Selves.

There is an excellent book called Working Identity by Herminia Ibarra. It's aimed at people of any age who know in their heart they want to do something else, but they are not sure what.

Like any good self-help book, it lays out 9 Steps to help potential transformation. It's a powerful and practical process.

Step No.3 is "imagine a range of possible future selves".

Let's say you are an accountant but secretly you want a more creative life. We are not suggesting that accountants cannot be creative. But you want something more.

The author, backed by mountains of data, says that the chances of you choosing your one true self unilaterally is vanishingly small. Much better to imagine 5 or 10 or 15 different potential future selves. And be as "adventurous and incoherent as you can. If you are an accountant don't put down as one of your future selves "Auditor." Or "Tax Consultant." Those are next step extensions of what you're doing today. The next rung on your ladder. We are looking for a new ladder.

The point of the exercise is to expand your thinking and challenge your paradigms.

What if we applied the idea to sustainability?

Too often, we limit ourselves to obvious next steps: recycling more, driving less, eating less meat. These are fine actions, but they're the equivalent of the accountant becoming an auditor.

They're safe. Incremental. Expected.

What if instead, we imagined radically different versions of our sustainable selves? What if the suburban homeowner didn't just install LED bulbs, but reimagined their quarter-acre as an experimental food forest? What if the marketing executive didn't just switch to a hybrid, but reinvented themselves as a community seed bank coordinator? What if the retired teacher didn't just join a climate action group, but became their neighbourhood's first repair coach, teaching others how to fix what they'd normally throw away?

The point isn't that any single one of these futures is right. The point is that by imagining multiple, even seemingly absurd possibilities, we break free from the prison of incremental thinking.

We stop asking What's next? and start asking What if?

Maybe you write down: Urban mushroom cultivator. Plastic-free shop owner. Community energy cooperative founder. Regenerative ocean farmer. Zero-waste event planner. Circular economy educator. The specifics matter less than the exercise of stretching your imagination until it squeaks.

Consider Eben Bayer, who combined his love of farming with engineering to grow packaging materials from mushrooms and turn it into a multi-million dollar business. Or Safia Minney, who left a career in marketing to launch People Tree, pioneering fair trade fashion well before sustainability was trendy. Or Rob Greenfield, who transformed from a marketing executive into a zero-waste educator who grows or forages all his own food.

A decade ago, their paths seemed absurd. Today, they're entrepreneurs.

Because here's what happens when you let yourself imagine multiple future selves: The impossible starts feeling possible. The radical starts feeling reasonable. And most importantly, you start seeing paths you never knew existed. Maybe you don't become any of these things—but you might become something equally surprising that emerges from allowing yourself to think beyond the obvious.

This isn't just personal transformation—it's how we transform society. Because the solutions we need won't come from doing slightly better versions of what we're already doing. They'll come from people brave enough to imagine entirely new ways of living, working, and relating to our planet.

All ideas seem ridiculous until they are done.

So grab a piece of paper. Write down ten possible sustainable future selves. Make at least five of them feel ridiculous.

Then ask yourself: What if they're not ridiculous at all? What if they're just ahead of their time?

What can you do by Friday?

Write down 9 possible future sustainable selves. Make the first 3 safe and obvious. Make the next 3 feel slightly uncomfortable. Make the last 3 feel completely absurd. Circle the one that makes you laugh out loud at its audacity. Then spend 30 minutes researching if anyone, anywhere, is already doing it. You might be surprised to find that your "absurd" future is already someone else's present. And if no one is doing it yet? Maybe that's not a sign it's impossible. Maybe it's a sign the world is waiting for you to make it possible.

MY POSSIBLE FUTURE SELVES

(Remember: Be bold. Be ridiculous. Be surprising.)

Before you start writing, ask yourself:

• What if money wasn't a constraint?

• What if you had all the skills and knowledge you needed?

• What if failure wasn't possible?

- What if your age didn't matter?
- What if you could start over completely?

1.

_____

2.

_____

3.

_____

4.

_____

5.

_____

6.

_____

7.

_____

8.

_____

9.

_____

10.

_____

What happens next?

Once you've written your list, don't judge it. Don't edit it. Instead:

Circle the three that make your heartbeat faster (even if they seem impossible; especially if they seem impossible)

Pick one to research this week. Just research. No commitment.

Find one person who's doing something vaguely similar & reach out to them

Share your wildest idea with someone who won't judge you

Remember: Every transformation starts with giving yourself permission to imagine it.

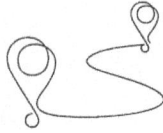

2050 is Not the Finish Line.

It's not just you. And it's not just the media. Things are getting worse.

The science suggests +2C might be the threshold. And 2050 might be a tipping point.

That might feel like half a lifetime away. It's not. It's closer than 1999.

It's easy to reframe those predictions or "targets" as worst case - like a college assignment deadline that we can cram for the night before.

They are not.

That may be best case. No one really knows. Apart from one incontrovertible fact – things are getting worse, and they are accelerating.

Based on the one-in-100-year weather events that appear to be happening every 100 days, we should not be counting on another 30 years of cushion.

There's a better word for forecast. A more accurate one.

Guess.

What can you do by Friday?

Find three photos: one from 1999, one from today, and one of a young person you care about. Place them side by side. The 1999 photo isn't ancient history - it's exactly as far behind us as 2050 is ahead. Let that sink in. Now look at that young person's photo and write beneath it: "This is what 2050 looks like." Because 2050 isn't some distant finish line - it's a real face, someone you love, who will live in the world we either changed or didn't. What story do you want them to tell about what we did in 2024?

Breaking the Bro Code.

"Dude, not you too with this climate stuff."

It's happy hour at the pub. Jim's rolling his eyes. Tom's chuckling into his whiskey.

Do you laugh along? Or do you speak up?

Here's the thing about the Bro Code: It's comfortable. It's easy. It's safe.

It's also a trap. Because deep down, you know the truth. Climate change isn't a hoax, or just a headline. It's not someone else's problem. And it's not going away by dissing it.

"Look, guys," you might say. "I'm not trying to be 'woke' here. I'm just kind of waking up."

The raised eyebrows. The subtle shift in the air.

"What do you mean, waking up?" Jim might ask, curiosity escaping through his scepticism.

This is your moment. Not to preach, but to lead.

"I mean, we've all seen the headlines. One in a 100-year storms every other week. All the fires. Adam can't insure his beach place anymore. It's real. It's a fu*king mess. And we - yeah, us - we can actually do something about it."

Tom leans in. "Like what? We're not exactly running oil companies here."

"Like switching to renewable energy for our homes. Investing in sustainable tech. Hell, even just choosing an electric car for the next upgrade."

"How about we take one truck camping this weekend not three"

You're not asking them to hug trees, live in caves or learn to like tofu. You're inviting them to be leaders, not followers, or bystanders.

Will you face resistance? Sure.

But some will listen. They'll ponder. They might take that Polestar for a test drive. They might even buy one.

That's how change happens. Not through grand speeches or policy changes, but through BBQ conversations over a beer. Through small examples. Through waking up and nudging others awake.

It's not about being woke. It's about being *awake*.

Because here's what the Bro Code doesn't tell you:

Real bros don't let bros destroy the fucking planet.

What can you do by Friday?

At your next hangout, share one specific thing you're doing about climate change - your solar quote, that EV test drive, whatever feels real to you. Don't preach, just plant the seed. Then offer to help a buddy take the same step. "Hey, want my solar guy's number? His quotes are free, and I learned a lot."

About Emily.

Planning isn't progress. It's procrastination.

Starting doesn't need endless planning. It needs an initial step. The first step is often inconvenient, wobbly, out of our comfort zone, and scary.

In our fight against climate change, immediate action trumps perfect plans.

Emily lives in a small, bustling city. Like many of us, she is deeply concerned about climate change.

She reads books, attends seminars, and fills her journal with plans to reduce her carbon footprint.

Yet, amidst all this planning, Emily knew she hadn't actually *done* anything. She was just as guilty as the politicians and corporations she often criticised.

Until one Saturday morning when she was walking to her local cafe. She noticed an elderly neighbour and her grandson planting a tree in their front yard.

It was a simple act, but it struck her. Here was someone taking direct action. Yesterday there was no tree. Now there is.

While she was still planning.

The next day, instead of driving to work, she took the bus.

She hadn't been on a bus since she left school. She had to download the transport app; she had to leave home early. She had to sit beside a person who smelled curious. She saw things she hadn't seen in 7 years of driving. She read 10 pages of her book.

It was a nuisance, and she loved it.

This was her tipping point. She learned that one tiny action is more powerful than months of planning.

Planning gives an illusion that we are making progress. But real change often comes from spontaneous actions that disrupt our routine thinking.

Emily's encounter with the lemon tree-planting neighbour disrupted her cycle of endless planning.

This is how movements are born - through imperfect action – that gather momentum and inspire others.

What can you do by Friday?

It's the actors, not the planners, who change the world.

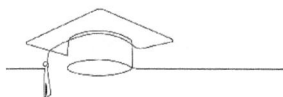

Oxford Musings.

The Ashmolean Museum in Oxford, founded in 1683, prides itself on being the oldest museum in the English-speaking world. Its collection is extensive to the point of infinity. From archaeology and anthropology, Roman jewellery, Hebrew scriptures, and the most gorgeous Mughal thousand-flower carpets, all form a coherent tapestry of knowledge.

Just a few yards away, the Museum of Natural History boasts "five million insects: over half a million fossils, rocks, and minerals".

Confronted with science, history, and humanities, two questions come to my mind. With the current loss of biodiversity and the dwindling of species, will these museums soon feel too large? Will their 22nd-century versions become relics of a bygone era? Or, on the contrary, will these museums evolve in the most captivating entertainment venues because the gap between the world our children will live in and the world these museums preserves will make a visit feel like a journey to a lost future?

Another question arises: Should we invest in disappearing species? What if, by betting on the destruction of our habitats, we could capitalize on rare, endangered species, buying them now and reselling them when their value will have skyrocketed based on exotic marketing trends, much like The Melanie Trump's crypto meme? Can we? Should we?

These are irrational thoughts. They are born of awe and panic. The awe of witnessing the vastness of our biosphere, and the panic of watching its collapse unfold before us.

What can you do by Friday?

History repeats itself. Where will you stand?

The entry wall of the Bodleian Library features a long list of names carved in marble. These philanthropists funded the conservation of knowledge.

Which stone, bark, or catalogue do you want your name written on?

Section 4.

You as a Business Leader

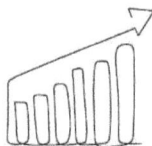

The Idiot's Guide to Sustainability Ambitions.

Let's face it, most businesses sustainability practice are like that one guy at the gym who swears he's "working on it," but hasn't picked up a single weight.

Enter the four stages of sustainability ambitions, a consultants dream for simplicity. With a few tweaks from us, we believe these four stages will be your secret weapon to assess just how serious your business is about climate action.

Are you in the pro zone, or still stuck in the locker room?

Use our tool at the decision table to enlighten your CEO about where the business truly stands—somewhere between good intentions and game-changing positions.

There's no shame in the answer. It just is time to take a good, hard look in the mirror.

Stage 1 - aka "You can't be serious"

Ah yes, stage 1, where your business does the bare minimum. You've got recycled paper in the photocopy room and your office cafeteria offers reusable flatware.

Well done. Very 1990.

We call these "non-strategic efforts", the heartwarming initiatives, that scream, "Hey, we're doing something!".

Token gestures, and just enough environmental compliance to say you're *technically* doing your part.

It's cute. But let's be real—it's not enough.

Stage 2 - aka "Try harder"

Stage 2 is where the progress happens... kind of.

You're doing more of the Stage 1 feel-good stuff, but now you're attempting to engage in some actual material efforts. You're not quite there, though.

Meaning if you are in the automobile industry you are NOT redesigning your cars into Electric vehicles just yet. You *may* have redesigned *some* of your products to manifest your good intentions.

You may have key sustainability metrics in place, even reduction targets on your greenhouse gas emissions and waste, but you don't yet have a solid detailed net zero transition plan across the full range of your business activities. Oh, and those investments you'll need to make it happen? Still not there.

That's where most businesses are today, stuck in between the past and the present, missing the fortitude to truly engage in what tomorrow promises to be. Dipping toes but not diving in the future.

Stage 3 -aka "Is it hurting yet?"

This is where the real deal begins.

You've started a thorough integration of environmental and social impact across your business.

You have a climate transition plan in place openly addressing your impact areas, with specific targets, resources, and, wait for it - costs clearly laid out.

In short, you know what to do and when, and this is driving measurable business performance. This is also requiring trade-offs, resources, data, and governance. Yes, it is hurting.

Sustainability isn't a pet project anymore; you're laying the foundation for long-term success.

Guess what? That's where the big players are making waves, where a growing share of businesses are driving bold actions AND reaping commercial benefits.

Sustainable business models? They don't need to be cool to talk about anymore—they're the key to thriving in the future economy.

Stage 4 - aka "You're smashing it."

Welcome to the major league. You've completely revamped your business ecosystem around sustainability and climate action. Bar none. You are creating new models that are radically challenging your industry status quo.

You are using data, technology, and industry collaboration to stay ahead of the curve.

That's where the real fight is, between the bold incumbents and the audacious pure players playing offense in the new net zero economy.

What can you do by Friday?

Define where you stand on the ambition ladder.

Understand where you can unlock true competitive value.

Think radically about the resources, investments, and bold steps that will catapult your business to the next stage of sustainability greatness.

3 I's

Inertia. Ignorance. Incertitude.

These are the enemies, the voices that harm our progress.

They creep around us like leeches at a potluck.

You'll poke them out, like a game of whack-a mole, believing you've cleared the deck of the infamous 3 I's.

But they'll resurface refreshed like fruit flies, emboldened by a budget cut, a political shift, a demonic woke scare, or an economic slowdown.

The 3 I's are not just obstacles; they are malevolent forces.

They cripple ambitions, shatter resilience, and corrode the hardiest souls.

They are eloquent, reassuring, controlling, and manipulative.

They use phrases like "let's stay focused", they'll bebop "our short-term objectives", they'll hold grandiloquent "simplify it". They will lull you into submission, and suffocate any attempt to move your legacy business into the net zero future.

This is what they will compulsively stop or slow down:

- Your investments for bold actions to seize the new opportunities of climate action.
- Your development of the data, engineering and services required to drive the net zero journey.
- Your business resources allocated to transitioning your products and services portfolio toward more sustainable options.
- Your deployment of clean technologies and the transformation of legacy assets lagging in climate performance.
- Your efforts to educate your entire organisation about the new mantra of responsible capitalism.

What can you do by Friday?

Be present, the journey won't be easy, but each decision you make moves you closer to the future we need.

"It is not the critic who counts; not the man who points out how the strong man stumbles, or where the doer of deeds could have done them better.

The credit belongs to the man who is actually in the arena.

Whose face is marred by dust and sweat and blood; who strives valiantly; who errs, who comes short again and again because there is no effort without error and shortcoming; but who does actually strive to do the deeds; who knows great enthusiasms, the great devotions.

Who spends himself in a worthy cause; who at the best knows in the end the triumph of high achievement, and who at the worst, if he fails, at least fails while daring greatly.

So that his place shall never be with those cold and timid souls who neither know victory nor defeat."

Theodore Roosevelt

Sorbonne, Paris, April 23, 1910

Green skills.

Green skills aren't just for climate scientists and renewable energy engineers. They're for doing every job, in every department, in a better, greener way.

Green skills are a mindset.

They are about how a person thinks and acts about the role the environment plays (or doesn't) in their approach to doing business.

Green skills do not require knowing the deep science of climate change; they're about understanding system thinking, and integrating new environmental knowledge in everyday work, no matter what your title is.

An always-on sustainability is the ultimate green skill— a way of thinking that can help companies make their economic activities not just profitable, but more environmentally sustainable.

It doesn't matter what role you are in, or where you are in your career. Green skills can be in finance, human resources, or operations.

If you want to make a difference you need to develop the green skills that your business needs to thrive in a net zero economy.

What can you do by Friday?

Build mindset. Dive in the fascinating knowledge required to live within our planetary boundaries.

Soak in market knowledge about the ever-growing flow of new net zero technologies, products. and services.

Understand the complexity of today's economic transition.

Embrace the future and make it green.

You are in the Oil Business.

Every day, billions of plastic cups, packaging, and containers are used across the globe; massive quantities of chemical fertilizers are dumped into farmland; billions of gallons of jet fuel are burned by planes circling the planet.

We live in a fossil fuel-based economy—a system whose brain, organs, and skeleton were painstakingly built over decades.

Whether we like it or not, this lethal model is about to go.

The world is accelerating toward a low-carbon future, driven by extreme weather events, new regulation, and a social demand for change.

Temporary headwinds do not shift the north star of this transition.

What does this mean?

It means you have an unprecedented opportunity to lead in this changing world.

Not by ideologically swapping brown for green, but by strategically guiding your business through a net zero transformation that builds equity.

By intelligently adopting the new low carbon, high performance solutions that are already here - and more cost-effective than their carbon-emitting fossil fuel counterparts.

By embedding climate into your business core operations and customer value proposition

Take the obvious wind and solar, for example. Between 2010 and 2020, the cost of solar electricity plummeted by nearly 90%. Onshore wind electricity dropped by more than 50%. That's how you can directly and immediately save money, by adopting the solutions that are already "in the money".

Sometimes, you need to integrate Green Design Principles to achieve better outcomes. Take for example the Ford River Rouge car factory in Detroit, once a brown field, is now a thriving centre of biodiversity after its restoration by American architect Bill McDonough. The factory redesign improved long-term asset value and the cost of running it.

As the world generates massive amounts of waste, think about the opportunity to transform organic waste into biogas through anaerobic digestion - which New York City implemented at scale, just last year.

Or the rise of micromobility options like electric scooters and bikes which is revolutionizing the automotive sector, setting new ecological standards.

These are examples of industry transformation taking place around us. Every sector, from construction to retail and agriculture, is undergoing similar deep structural transformations, and are filled with opportunities to reduce emissions, cut costs, and drive innovation.

Investing today to yield returns tomorrow.

What can you do by Friday?

The next step is yours.

Transition your procurement, investments, and resources toward a new model where fossil fuel resources are displaced and carbon taxes finance zero-emission alternatives.

Ask the right questions to ChatGPT, or the dozens of platforms using AI to optimise our net zero trajectory.

This isn't about environmental responsibility. It's about making bold profitable moves.

Pay Your Dues.

Think about it like this. When you came across one of those free community book boxes in your neighbourhood, do you take all the books at once and leave the shelves empty? No, you don't. You take a couple of books and leave the rest for others. You even bring your own books for other to enjoy.

It's the same with those fruit stalls on the roadside. When you take some of the fruits on display, and no one is watching, you still leave a little cash in the money box, don't you?

Why should carbon emissions be any different?

Anyone who takes from the atmosphere should pay for it. Our natural resources aren't free—just like the fruits or books we enjoy.

Whether it's the energy to heat our homes, the fuel to drive our cars, or the products we buy, carbon emissions are embedded in it all.

They come at a cost that should be factored in. That's what a carbon tax is designed to do.

What can you do by Friday?

Well, pay your dues.

Why you Should Talk with the Accounting Bot.

There is a funny tendency in the boardroom.

Whenever we speak about climate action and sustainability, most executives become slightly uncomfortable. They may chuckle, nod solemnly, or claim they're paying deep attention, and then inevitably say, "Yes, this is the right thing to do."

This, my friends, gets you nowhere.

The second the sky gets cloudy and economic conditions turn sour - like they are doing at the time of this writing - leadership's tone changes from humanistic aspiration to cold accounting bots.

Getting back to business fundamentals become the resounding calls.

So delete doing The 'right thing'. Instead, talk about cash, dollar, euro, yuans, pesos, or whatever currency makes your world go round.

Speak about the making and allocation of capital. Break down the impact of climate on business activity.

Embrace money, make it your friend. Use the language that is universally understood by every pedestrian soul walking the earth.

At present McKinsey estimates that 65% annual spending goes into high emissions assets, meaning the type of assets that directly worsen the climate crisis, essentially by burning coal, oil, and destroying our planet one way or another. This is not going away, certainly not under a Trump administration singing drill baby drill at every rally.

Yet, in the scenario where business and society reorganise intelligently to limit the damage of climate change, McKinsey predicts this pattern will reverse: 70% of capital allocation will be directed to low emissions assets.

In fact, companies, customers and investors are already spending hundreds of billions of dollars on sustainable products and services in infrastructures, energy, food, transport, hospitality, and so forth.

Irrelevant of the political flavour of the month, your sector of activity will be disrupted, and you need to understand the timeline, scale and sheer size of that disruption.

What can you do by Friday?

#1: Sound the alarm of market disruption.

#2: Tap into the extensive literature published by some of the brightest analysts globally.

#3: Detail the specific trajectory of sectoral transformation, wherever you are, whichever industry you work in.

#4: Put targets, dates, and investments against it.

#5: Make your company's CFO an ally to your ambitions.

This is a transformation journey. You are starting it now.

"How did you go bankrupt? Two ways. Gradually, then suddenly."

Ernest Hemingway, The Sun Also Rises

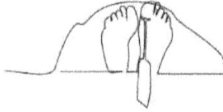

Over My Dead Body.

We know how it works.

You're missing Q3 numbers. You have to save money. You reach for the trusty cost saving levers:

- Headcount.

- Marketing.

- Business class travel.

- ~~Sustainability initiatives.~~

Over my dead body. And the dead body of your unborn granddaughter. The one you just wrote to, Emma.

Go on record now and say that you are not sacrificing future generations for the sake of the annual report.

The sustainability budget stays.

What can you do by Friday?

Make sure all sustainability initiatives stay.

Get rid of the coffee cups.

I'll never forget the scene.

I am walking through our corporate cafeteria with our CEO.

A big sharp man dressed in black, British breed, fast walker, with a copious amount of impatience.

Next to him I look French, well intentioned, and hesitant,

He throws a challenge at me: "get rid of the disposable coffee cups". He adds "by next Monday".

Here is my first mandate, as the newly appointed Chief Sustainability Officer of New Zealand's largest retail group, a multi-billion dollar business.

"Remove the disposable coffee cups". Barely the dream job I had envisioned.

What bursts to my mind is of Olympian clarity: I'm the best paid coffee cup manager in this business. A medal of honour I do not want to pin to my lapel.

Reflect.

What I was lacking at that time was vision.

The vision that if you astutely reach people where it matters to them you open a line of communications, which you can leverage to your most noble intentions.

Said differently, if you want to accelerate climate action around you, do not ever start by going to the global thermostat, alone, pretending your herculean ego will change the course of humanity.

It won't.

Who will? An army, a team, a movement. In the case of our business, 12,000 team members.

Removing disposable coffee cups from our corporate office cracked open the door of a conversation that never stopped.

12,000 team members became ardent supporters of making small changes that matter.

And small changes quickly turn into big.

This is what we could achieve immediately after the coffee cups experience:

- Make the business the first large retailer in Australasia to become carbon neutral.
- Commit to sell products using 100% sustainable packaging or certified ingredients.
- Switch 100% of our corporate cars to EVs.
- Be the first large business in New Zealand to switch all our electricity needs to solar energy.

- Launch the largest e-waste and plastic waste recycling programs in the country.
- And the list goes on.

A small act snowballed into an utterly complete transformation.

What Can you Do by Friday?

First, remove these damn disposable coffee cups. Compostable or not, they are useless.

Second, please open the communications line with your team members.

Third, recognise that eating an elephant is something you do one bite at a time.

Fourth, start writing that list of opportunities you have, already in your control, to reduce your carbon emissions and save money.

Fifth, execute, now, by tomorrow and Friday alike.

One At a Time.

An old man was walking along a beach that was littered with thousands of starfish that had been washed ashore by the high tide.

As he walked, he came upon a young girl who was eagerly throwing the starfish back into the ocean, one by one.

Puzzled, the man looked at the girl and asked what she was doing. Without looking up from her task, the girl simply replied, "I'm saving these starfish, Sir."

The old man chuckled aloud, "But there are thousands of starfish on this beach and only one of you. What difference can you possibly make?"

The girl picked up another starfish, gently tossed it into the water and turning to the man, said, "It made a difference to that one!"

What can you do by Friday?

Do what you can with what you have.

Unless someone like you cares a whole awful lot, nothing is going to get better. It's not.

Dr Seuss, The Lorax

Rewild your Business.

What can you do by Friday is a metaphor, an enthusiastic call for urgent action in a world that lingers in complacency.

But not everything can be done in a single week.

Rewilding your business is a process of transformation that requires patience and resilience, especially when the winds are blowing in opposite direction. When you need to overcome the Inertia, Incertitude and Ignorance, the 3's of evil and the weaponisation of climate action and ESG by politics that ignore our planet sentient's reality, our ecological interdependency that should compel us to care.

Rewilding your business is about reintroducing principles, practices and strategies that reconnect it the natural world - with nature-positive actions and long-term ecological balance.

Rewilding your business should be fact-based and opportunity led, not driven by risk mitigation or legal compliance, nor ideological and ignorant of the market forces.

Rewilding is inspired by a collective vision of what we need to balance economic growth and environmental progress.

Rewilding your business opens the flow gates to new commercial opportunities inspired by how we can flourish in a new regenerative net zero economy, one where business and nature are not separate but interwoven, creating values in ways never done before. It is an economy where the market forces and economic rationales align with the health of the planet, and where growth respects the planetary boundaries

To rewild your business is to become part of the future—a future that recognizes business's role in restoring ecological health, nurturing new opportunities, and creating lasting value for both people and planet.

So, what can you do by Friday?

Progress, not perfection.

You can use the checklist below as a framework to progress through, one checkbox at a time.

1. Products

Start by measuring your products and services against climate, biodiversity, and circularity criteria.

Identify their impact throughout their entire lifecycle—during manufacturing, usage, and post-usage.

- **Action Step:** Conduct a materiality assessment to pinpoint product impact hotspots against climate and biodiversity, or the broader planetary boundaries.
- **Examples:** Unilever's Sustainable Living Brands, IKEA's Circular Business Model, Nike's "Move to Zero," and Apple's carbon-neutral products such as the Apple Watch.
- **Our Insight:** Sustainability goes hand in hand with great design.

2. Processes & Systems

Rewild your operations by reducing emissions across processes in transportation, manufacturing, logistics, and procurement.

- **Action Step:** Track emissions at every step, from raw materials to energy use and packaging.
- **Examples:** Patagonia's supply chain, Walmart's Project Gigaton, and Bureo's circular economy practices.
- **Our Insight:** Technology helps, but the key to the transformation is aligning your entire ecosystem—suppliers, partners, stakeholders of all kind, and internal systems—with your sustainability goals.

3. Positions & Engagement

Clarity and transparency are key to communicating your climate goals. The "Why" you're doing it.

- Action Step: Clearly state your goals, integrate them into reports, and engage both internal and external stakeholders. Build leadership though partnerships.
- Examples: Patagonia's environmental advocacy and MAC Cosmetics social positions.
- Our Insight: Build strong alliances that reflect your values, and lead through collaboration. Such strategies can bring significant benefits.

4. People & Culture

Make sustainability a core part of your company culture. Why? Because as the adage says, Culture eats Strategy for breakfast.

- Action Step: Hire, develop, and reward people committed to sustainability.
- Examples: Salesforce and Google reward employees contributing to climate goals.
- Our Insight: Leadership should model sustainability, integrating it into everyday decisions and performance metrics.

5. Performance Metrics

Incorporate climate risks into decision-making and investments.

- Action Step: Use tools like the TCFD to track climate-related disclosures and integrate climate metrics into capital allocation.
- Examples: BlackRock's focus on climate-related risks in investments, Enel's prioritization of renewable energy projects.
- Our Insight: Monitoring and reporting climate data is crucial, but action is what truly drives change.

In one year, you'll look back and be astounded at how far you've come on the rewilding journey.

Not overnight. Over time.

$$(1.00)^{365} = 1.$$
$$(1.01)^{365} = 37.8$$

That 0.01 makes all the difference.

Every day, a choice. Every choice, an impact.

Small, Yes. Insignificant, No.

Think of climate change like a big gnarly, stuck in the mud boulder. Everyone looks at it as they walk by. Immovable

But that's not true.

Here's the secret: It's already moving. Slowly. Inevitably. The question is, which direction?

Start small. Really small.

Turn off a light. Skip meat for a meal. Walk instead of drive.

These aren't world-changing acts. They're not meant to be.

They're meant to be habitual. Repeatable. Daily.

Because here's the thing about habits: They grow.

That light you turned off? Soon it's all the lights. That meatless meal? It becomes meatless Mondays. That walk? It turns into biking to work. And selling your second car.

Small actions, repeated, become lifestyles.

And lifestyles? They become movements. They're contagious.

Your neighbour notices your solar panels. Your coworker asks about your bike. Your kids start sorting the garbage (without being asked).

Ripples. Spreading outward.

Every action is a vote. People notice. Companies notice.

Buy local, they stock more local goods. Choose electric, they make more electric options. Avoid plastic, they find alternatives.

Your choices shape the world.

But here's the real magic: Compounding doesn't just affect your actions. It affects you.

Each choice reinforces your commitment. Each action strengthens your resolve. Each day, you become more of who you want to be.

You are no longer someone who comments.

You become a person who cares. Who acts. Who leads.

And leadership? It's not about grand gestures. It's about consistent action. Daily commitment. Childlike enthusiasm.

You become a mentor. A living example of what's possible.

Others will follow. Not because you told them. But because you showed them.

This is how culture shifts. How it has always shifted.

Not with a massive push. But with tiny nudges.

Every day. Every choice. Every action.

And before you know it, that boulder? It's rolling. Slowly. Then faster. Then it's unstoppable.

All because you decided made one small change. And then another. And another.

This is the power of compounding.

It starts with you. Today.

What will your first small step be?

Take a step. Then take another. Others will join you.

What can you do by Friday?

Pick the smallest possible sustainable action you can think of.

Now make it even smaller.

Write it on a sticky note, along with '×365'.

Put it somewhere you'll see it daily.

Do it once today. Just once. And again tomorrow. Every time you do it, put a tiny dot on the note.

By Friday, you'll have several dots. The note stays up for a year.

This isn't about the action anymore - it's about watching your dots compound. It's about becoming a dot-maker.

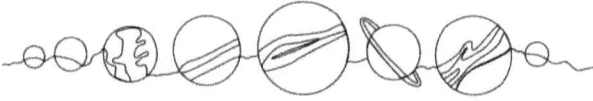

Life on Earth.

Did you watch "The Martian"?

Mark Watney, played by a boyish Matt Damon, is stranded alone on Mars. Left with few options to survive, he repurposes his feces as ingredients of a makeshift fertilization system. Injecting vital nutrients into the soil, he engineers a new lifeline: a small crop of potatoes.

Have you considered your own options?

Adaptation to climate change has begun. It may not be as extreme as The Martian proposes, but the logic applies. We now live on Earth 2.0, a riskier ecosystem resulting from decades of extreme environmental stress. Every single activity you, your business, and your community undertake needs adaptation.

Take the example of the urban planners, now building sponge cities capable of managing flood risks. Wetlands, forests, rain gardens and ponds are used to store and filter water.

Urban planners do not work alone on Mars. They work in tandem with municipalities, policymakers, entrepreneurs, investors, and community members. They manage biodiversity, habitats, energy, and people flow.

Shanghai, Beijing Nairobi, Auckland, Singapore and Miami are now sponge cities.

The scenario of their work is worth every Oscar.

What can you do by Friday?

First, Think hard, but not for long. It took 8 years and 2 months between President John F. Kennedy announcing the goal to land an American on the moon and the time when Apollo 11 successfully landed there.

Second, ask your local council, your town, do you have a plan, and how is that plan protecting you, your home, and your family.

Third, meet with your corporate board, your CEO, your leadership. Ask them who is managing business risk, and if that risk includes climate change. What solutions are they putting in place? If they stare at you blankly, show them the Martian.

Don't Despair.

Whether you lean left, right, or cling to the ever-dwindling centre, it's hard to deny that recent political events around the world have thrown a wrench into climate action.

The rhetoric is loud, previous promises are being broken, and the distractions are relentless. It's easy to feel like we're careening down a track toward a future that seems a little darker, a little hotter, and a lot more uncertain.

But here's the thing: Don't despair. Don't retreat into cynicism. It's time to stand up, not step back.

Some are calling it a disaster, proof that we've lost the plot. Some say it's just the natural cycle of politics, a pendulum that will swing back again in time. Others argue that the economy must come first, and that jobs and growth take priority over clean air and a stable climate.

If you're feeling helpless, it's because you're looking at the wrong scoreboard. The real action isn't happening in big white buildings full of lobbyists and hot air. It's happening in our choices, our wallets, in our backyards. It's easy to blame politicians for stalling climate action—it's harder to admit that we have a role in this too.

It's time to push a little harder, to put your hand up, to dig in deeper. Because every small action you take now is an antidote to the despair that creeps in when the headlines don't go our way.

Here's what the headlines won't tell you: While politicians debate, solar panels are getting cheaper. While talking heads argue, electric vehicles are getting better. While pundits predict doom, innovative companies are finding new ways to capture carbon, reduce waste, and revolutionize recycling. The future is being written by people who refused to wait for permission from Washington, or Brussels, or Downing Street.

Think about this: Every time you make a climate-conscious choice, you're not just reducing your carbon footprint—you're casting a vote with your actions. You're sending a signal to the market that there's demand for better solutions. You are part of a quiet revolution that is happening right under everyone's nose.

The truth is, political winds shift. But physics doesn't care about politics. The atmosphere doesn't negotiate. The ocean doesn't compromise. They respond to actions, not words. And that's our superpower—the ability to act, regardless of what's happening in the halls of power.

So let's get on with it.

TURNING DESPAIR INTO ACTION.

This week:

1. Make One Simple Bold Move

Join a community garden

Start a neighbourhood repair café

Propose a novel sustainability initiative at work

   Pick one. Do it well before you're ready.

2. Find Your Local Heroes

Look up environmental groups in your area

Attend a city council meeting (you might be surprised what goes on there)

Connect with a sustainability-focused business nearby – see how it works.

They're out there. Find them. Join them. Encourage them.

3. Create Your Own Ripple

Teach someone a simple sustainability skill you have

Share a success story on social media – write it well, how you tell the story matters.

Start a conversation about climate solutions (not problems) at work. What is another business already doing that yours could do easily?

Remember: ideas are cheap and easy. Action is what matters. While the world debates climate action, you can create climate progress. Your move.

Need some more inspiration? Try this:

What local problem pisses you off?

What solution(s) would you love to see? Maybe you don't know – but someone will.

What's stopping you from starting?

What's a tiny first step you could take – by Friday?

Write your answers below: ___

Do No4. Not next week. By Friday.

Who is in the Empty Chair?

According to Amazonian legend - the company, not the river - critical meetings always have an empty chair at the table.

A chair for the Amazon customer. A reminder of who makes the decisions that matter.

It sounds a bit woo-woo, but it actually works. You need to try it

So many meetings are held in a perception bubble worshipping a 35 slide PowerPoint that was curated to impress rather than enlighten.

The empty chair can be a circuit breaker.

Imagine if we applied this concept to our sustainability discussions. What if every decision we made had an empty chair watching on, representing future generations, the environment, or even our own health and well-being?

This simple yet profound shift in perspective could be the key to moving from performative sustainability to genuine, impactful action.

The Power of the Empty Chair

The idea of the empty chair is not a corporate gimmick; it can be a powerful tool for fostering empathy and foresight. By representing an empty chair in meetings, or at the dinner table, we remind ourselves of the broader impact of our choices.

Put your granddaughter in the chair. Or their granddaughter. Or their granddaughter.

This simple practice encourages us to think beyond immediate benefits and consider the long-term consequences for those who come after us.

The empty chair is more than just a symbol; it is a powerful tool for fostering empathy, foresight, and sustainability. By incorporating this practice into our meetings, homes, and decision-making processes, we can ensure that the needs and well-being of future generations are at least considered.

What can we do by Friday?

Embrace the empty chair, and let it guide you to pause and consider those not in the room.

Care enough, but not too much.

Mark Manson made us realise that "you only have so many fucks to give". Don't throw them away needlessly.

It's odd that in a book that is trying to nudge you relentlessly towards caring more about the environment, and what you can do to help climate change, that we would tell you not to care too much.

We do not want you to have a hot steamy all-in affair with sustainability – even though that sounds kind of fun. We want you to have a long dull marriage.

If you've spent time at the gym trying to build a 6 pack or a Kardashian bum, you will know consistency is far more important than intensity.

A little bit every day. Forever.

As Charlie Munger, the legendary investor, said the most important thing about harnessing the power of compounding effort is "not to disrupt it unnecessarily".

The most important thing about your personal sustainability practice is ironically its sustainability. Far better to commit to small changes that you can reliably and consistently perform, rather than "committing" to eating lettuce, wearing hemp underwear, and being sterilised to avoid the burden of personally increasing the population.

That does not negate the need for ambition. You could do one sit-up every single day for the next 1000 years and you will still not have that 6 pack.

The sweet spot is to choose ambitious changes that you can more easily commit to. Choosing an electric vehicle next time you buy a car, or insisting on solar panels on your next building project are good examples of ambitious changes that are easy to commit to.

A one-time decision. Long-term sustainable benefit. Easy.

But they don't have to be significant one-off decisions. Look at your decision-making as a personal algorithm. When X happens I do Y.

For any work-in-progress meeting of less than 3 hours, I will avoid the travel and dial in virtually.

When offered the opportunity of tap water I will always choose tap water over bottled water.

I will delete Temu from my phone because I buy stuff I don't want, and it scars the planet.

No, none of these small actions are going to save the planet. But they will save you an awful lot of time and effort with your decision-making and light that daily trip to the gym they do add up.

What can we do by Friday?

If you can't make those relatively easy decisions then don't pretend that you care, because you don't.

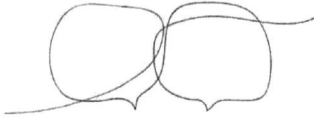

Green Shoots.

It starts with a seed.

Not a physical seed, but an idea. A spark of curiosity. A question.

"Why does this matter?"

Its where the best education begins. Not with answers, but with questions.

As parents, we plant these seeds daily. At the dinner table. On walks. In the car.

"Why do we have to bring our own bags? Dad never remembers to."

"Because it helps the planet. Want to know how?"

At work, our role is different, and sometimes harder because you don't make all the decisions. You're the gardeners of organizational culture.

Your actions speak louder than your emails. When you prioritise sustainability, others notice. They follow.

Teachers (and we are all teachers) don't teach – they create curiosity.

It's not about reciting facts. It's about building wonder and exploration.

"What if we designed cities like forests?"

"How do we make energy from ocean waves?"

Business leaders, you're the fertile soil. You provide resources, create opportunities.

Internships focused on green innovation. Mentorship programs for eco-entrepreneurs.

Community organizers, you're the pollinators. You spread ideas, connect people.

Local clean-up days. Workshops on sustainable living. You make abstract concepts tangible.

Children, you might think you're just learning. But you're teaching too.

Your enthusiasm is contagious. Your questions challenge old assumptions.

"Why can't all cars be electric?" "What if we built houses from mushrooms?"

This is how change happens. Not through lectures, but through living examples.

It's a collective effort. A web of interactions.

Each question asked, each idea shared, each action taken - they all matter.

They shape minds. Change behaviors. Influence policies.

This is eco-education. It's not confined to classrooms.

It happens everywhere. All the time. With everyone.

It's not about cramming for tests. It's about reimagining our world.

So plant those seeds. Nurture that curiosity. Celebrate those questions.

Because the next generation isn't just learning about a greener world.

They're creating it.

And it starts with you. Today. Right now.

What can we do by Friday?

What small seed are you going to plant today?

Speak Clearly, Or Not at All.

Better to be small and specific than big and vague.

Vague ambitions are a problem. They can easily give us a sense of achievement and satisfaction without delivering any real results. Vagueness makes us stumble on our path to action.

I will eat less junk food is not a plan. We will run a more sustainable supply chain is not a plan. We will help our customers be more sustainable is not a plan.

Fine words like diversity and sustainability mean nothing without an actionable plan. Indeed they can be worse than nothing because they create a false sense of progress.

The difference between vagueness and focus is what separates great from mediocre.

Nothing great was ever achieved intentionally without a specific plan. Your plan might change, in fact it almost certainly will, but without a plan there will be no specific action. And without specific action there can be no progress.

Unfortunately, a specific plan is hard work compared with a vague ambition. Running a marathon is quite a different thing from shouting out that you are going to run a marathon at 7 minutes past midnight on New Year's Eve.

It requires focus and detail. Even Winston Churchill who was famous for his sweeping oration viscerally understood that every grand claim had to be backed up by the requisite amount of detail.

2500 years ago, Socrates understood the power of focused thought when he stood in the early morning Athens marketplace and asked his fellow citizens what they were trying to achieve with their lives. They would routinely give grand answers: "justice" or "courage" or "beauty" or "art". Socrates would respond not by agreeing or disagreeing but by asking them what they meant by justice or courage or art or beauty.

Rarely could his fellow Athenians clarify.

Today the answers might be different but often the vagueness remains. I want to get fit. I want to lose weight. I want to be more present for my partner. I want to be a good role model for my children. I want to spend less time on social media.

None of those are wrong. Nor will any of them lead to meaningful outcomes.

There is a central idea here for sustainability.

If you claim to live a "sustainable life" it is no more or less than an ancient Greek claiming to live a just or courageous life.

In other words, it's practically useless.

When it comes to living a sustainable life – Sweeping vague statements is one of our most dogged adversaries.

What can we do by Friday?

Be specific. Say what you mean and mean what you say.

Do Less Than You Can.

In 1999 I attended a gala fundraiser in Sydney on behalf of Nike.

The guest speaker was Bob Geldof. He was in peak "fuck you" mode.

While everyone was in black tie he was in his usual scruffy uniform of opshop jacket, unwashed jeans, and homeless sneakers. Being Bob Geldof.

I loved him.

25 years later I can't remember most of what he said.

Until the last few sentences – which I remember verbatim.

He closed by saying to the smug, well-lubricated and fat-walleted group of Sydney's masters of the universe, in his lazy but machine gun-fast Irish:

"Tonight, I ask one thing. And one thing only.

Give less than you can, but a lot more than you fucking want to."

If you were deciding how much to invest in your company's sustainability programme - do not listen to your customers. They have a lot on their mind and frankly don't care about you, or what you do.

Do it because it's important. Do it because you have to.

Do it because you *can*.

And like Bob Geldof said give less than you can. and more than you fucking want to.

Because it matters far more than a couple of points of consumer preference and a few fleeting lines in your annual report.

What can we do by Friday?

Look at your next big purchase - that kitchen remodel, the new car, whatever.

Now add 20% to your budget, earmarked purely for making it climate-smart.

Not because it's sensible. Not because it's profitable. Because you fucking can.

Ominous Black.

This morning, lingering in a dark mood caused by compulsive news reading, I reached an ineffable conclusion.

Addressing the seismic reality of climate change - while navigating political choices and managing the day's pedestrian urgencies - can't be done coherently.

Not by myself. Not alone.

Not by anyone alone.

There is always a dissonance between beliefs, desires, fears and ambitions. The world is chaotic and dangerous, even though glimpses of progress exist in rotating corners of the universe.

Yet, like ants, we carry on our routines while our mind zooms in and out from ground levels to cosmic altitudes to consider the fate of humanity without ever being able to adjust the focal lens of what the future holds.

2050 is the new 30. Crypto, a gangster coin acclaimed by anarchists, nihilists and child traffickers, is adopted by central banks.

The Garden of Earthly Delights, by Hieronymus Bosch, depicts Desire, Folly and Morality across three panels: Paradise, Earthly pleasures, and Damnation. Picking one out of the three would be tempting, but they come as a package deal—just like the Shein haul videos your daughter binges before she buys another round of seven head-to-toe looks for the week, one per day.

You'll accuse your daughter of indulgence, - Bosh's Central Panel - sensory pleasures, hedonistic, without regard for consequences, dumpsters of textiles piling up in wasteland, while passionate start-ups demonstrate the new construction bricks made of textile cutouts that will build up the next student dormitories. Ikea, yo yeah.

Damnation, I cannot literally threaten your daughter of damnation without you pausing for a breather. I'll skip. I'll roll up back to collective inaction. Not your daughter. Not Emily. Not the hundreds of thousands protesting and asking for better choices, not the millions on the front line of climate change. But many others, yes, including those still allowing oil and gas companies, automobile car executives, and industry climate laggards to continue business as usual.

The rightmost panel depicts hell and punishment, our human excess and immorality. Temperature increases, natural disasters occur, and ecosystems collapse. One catastrophe at a time, hundreds died last month in Valencia, with just enough buffer time for us to forget the latest school shooting. Drill, baby drill.

It is not your daughter's fault. It's someone else you know —someone who missed their moment to intervene. That someone who once again missed the millisecond of moral intervention, that elusive particle humanity was graced with, and yet misses to activate so often. We get distracted, like the characters of Bosch's central panel. Personal pleasures, countries, and institutions. Eight hours of sleep turned into twenty-four.

Marine Le Pen, our national far-right demagogue, is accusing the French court of threatening democracy.

I didn't need Bosch painting to accept who we are. Dark moods are dark. Dark moods have their place—they can activate the divine light.

Back to panel one, two, and three.

Cop29 in Baku. Exxon Mobile's CEO is interviewed on Bloomberg Green, one of my go-to podcasts to track where we stand on climate action. "The world needs more oil. I am in the money-making business, not in the business of reducing the world's appetite for oil."

Point taken. What would have I said?

What Can We Do by Friday?

We can resist despair, embrace collaboration, and continue the journey. Each step is a step away from damnation and toward hope.

Together, we can rewrite Bosch's triptych with a brighter ending.

We can advocate for green policies and build the business case for clean, low-impact products, technologies and services.

We can lead business to do what it is supposed to do, make the world a better place.

We can move from competition to collaboration (thank you, Paul Polman) or do Kumbaia.

We can discuss it with our friends and colleagues, managers and directors, children and neighbours. They all care.

And snarl at those who still believe that fumes puking petrol cars are the symbol of modern living.

Wash and repeat.

Some like it Hot

The story goes like this.

In 2022, the UK experienced a heatwave like no others. A heatwave which, when experienced on a bicycle late at night, makes you feel like someone is holding a blow dryer up your face. A heatwave strong enough to shut down airports and railways, and make ice cream melt on kids' fingers in less time than they can bear. The type of heatwave that messes up with your organs, like a pint of gin and tonic on an empty stomach. A New Dehli type of heat wave.

Forty-degree heat is something few British people have experienced before. But please, move further east. Turn up the heat. Mecca, Saudi Arabia. White facades of clay, worshipping the Almighty during the holy hajj. Last summer, 53 degrees killed 1,301 pilgrims, not of God fear, but of heat stroke.

Back to England and its forty degrees. There is something eerie about complaining about a hot summertime when you are a skinny pale girl from Manchester or a chubby red-hair boy from Liverpool and all you've wanted was the chance to escape the Uk's grey cloudy sky.

3,000 excess deaths later. A shock to the collective system. Last year was the hottest year on record and next year will be the same.

Headlines are piling up. They're not about hurricanes, typhoons or wildfires. They're about nameless, invisible, deadly, and increasingly common heatwaves. Heatwaves that make us want to patch the world with air conditioning systems.

When the temperature reaches 35 degrees, just 5 degrees below the 40 degrees the subjects of the Crown experienced and if humidity kicks in, you get what scientists call wet-bulb temperatures, a point where the body sweating fails, leading to organ shutdown. In its ominous Climate Fiction novel *Ministry for the Future*, Kim Stanley Robinson describes a wet-bulb heatwave taking place in an Indian town in 2034. Millions perish. The world watches impassively. The Ministry for the Future is formed. It includes a shadow cabinet that uses direct action to target those profiting from burning fossil fuels.

What Can You do by Friday?

Step 1: Buy a share in Aramco. It is worth $7.43 (August 28 2024). Based in Saudi Arabia, Aramco is the largest oil and gas company in the world, responsible for 5% of total greenhouse gas emissions. It also sits on the largest oil reserves in the world. It is the least invested in renewable energy and decarbonisation of all the major oil and gas companies.

Step 2: Vote for Climate-related proposals. As a shareholder (of one share), you can vote on resolutions that require the company to reduce its greenhouse gas emissions.

Step 3: Ask hard questions directly to the board and management during the AGM. Use it to raise concerns about the company's environmental practices and push for commitments to renewable energy. Saudi is a mighty country with a mighty Prince. And a vision to turn away from the fossil fuel economy. A nudge in the right direction will encourage them get there faster.

Step 4: follow the similar shareholder activist work done at scale by the likes of Climate Action 100+, As You Sow, or Ceres. Engage with the likes of BP, Exxon, Shell, and Total, and continue to encourage these energy behemoths to do what they already know is the right thing to do: to transition their business for a net zero economy.

Kumbaya.

We each have our own tested techniques to convince friends and colleagues that our view of the world is the most logical and wise.

Metaphorically speaking, my favourite techniques involve using a hammer and a chisel to sculpt new beliefs in my audience's frontal lobe. Occasionally, I switch the hammer for one of these megaphones protestors use to deafen opponents.

These tools are my own way of convincing audiences that climate action is not only the right thing to do but also the profitable way to succeed in the new modern green economy, where clean technologies abound, and fortunes are made.

I have occasionally used props. For example, during my last tenure as the head of sustainability for a mass-market retail group, I dropped the content of our headquarters' trash bin on the boardroom table to convince our CEO that our 12,000 team members were avid recyclers. "C'mon, pal, you can't ignore what our team members tell us. Where there is demand, there is business."

These techniques are the techniques of a techno-optimist, a market fundamentalist, a good news peddler who believes that business can fix the world, that climate change is a technical problem we will solve by technical means with appropriate policies to drive their development.

Nothing wrong with that. At least not from afar.

Using that logic-based approach, we have gone a long way. For example, since 1990, the UK has cut its greenhouse gas emissions by 53%, and the economy has grown by 8% This shows how a leading economy can reduce greenhouse gas emissions while still experiencing economic growth.

This approach can apply to countries and businesses alike. It can apply to you, say if you switch your daily beef burger for beans or splurge for the new Chinese-made EV you can now buy for less than 30,000 Euros.

Logic-based solutions work.

To a point.

A 3.3-degree point

A pointless, frustrating, insufficient, hot and dangerous 3.3-degree point, which is the current temperature increase estimated by En-Roads, the temperature simulation tool developed by MIT.

3.3 degrees is more than double the 1.5-degree target of temperature increase that scientists have deemed safe for our kids. It comes with a full package, which includes the loss of biodiversity, the plastification of ocean life, and hundreds of thousands of victims of air pollution a year.

Techno-optimism works—until it doesn't. It takes us to a frontier between a world where climate action is limited because it is built on compromises, where the desire to transform is often held back by competing, logic-based arguments that prioritise caution over bold action.

So, what should we do?

We should move to what will sound like a funny concept to most of us: Love, beauty, and unity. Kumbaya.

Kumbaya is a social movement. It is the reconnection between the rational enlightenment enabled by extraordinary scientific progress and the unknown. It is the quest for a world where a fundamentally different type of culture powers decisions. The type of culture that results in Yvon Chouinard, Patagonia CEO, giving his corporate shares worth hundreds of millions of dollars to nature. A culture grounded away from the competitive market and into a new form of collaboration.

Harvard University Professor Rebecca Henderson calls this new age the age of Homo Reciprocans, as opposed to Homo Economicus. I call it Kumbaya. Why? Because I like it. Because I have seen Kumbaya with my own eyes without understanding its might.

I have seen the ceremonies and crop harvesting under the moon cycle, the rituals with nature and the Maori Whakapapa, a fundamental concept representing genealogy or lineage, a way of understanding identity, history, and relationships with our land and the cosmos. Whakapapa connects us to our ancestors, our environment, and our natural world, embodying the idea that all life is interconnected.

I have seen the dignity of the Indigenous tribes walking the aisles of the negotiations at the COP Climate Summits, carrying an outstanding beauty that reconnects the mundane with the divine. We have all seen the extraordinary beauty of the images captured by the James Webb Space Telescope. We are touching the origin of life. It goes beyond the limits of mathematical logic.

When I asked Paul Polman, the number one advocate for business sustainability leadership, what we should do by Friday, he suggested, "We should move from competition to cooperation". He meant we should do Kumbaya.

What Can You Do by Friday?

We can rebalance the rational with the magical and accept the vastness of the unknown.

We can embrace The Inner Development Goals (IDGs), which are proposed to support individuals and organisations in cultivating the inner qualities to exponentially progress sustainability and meet the United Nations Sustainable Development Goals.

The Inner Development Goals highlight the role of personal development in solving complex global challenges like climate change, inequality, and poverty.

The framework is structured around five dimensions:

1. Being: Focuses on cultivating inner peace, resilience, and self-awareness. This involves mindfulness and emotional balance.

2. Thinking: Encourages cognitive development, critical thinking, and an open mindset. It includes systems thinking, essential for solving complex problems.

3. Relating: Emphasizes the ability to foster relationships built on empathy, compassion, and communication. This helps individuals and teams work with a deep understanding of others' perspectives.

4. Collaborating: Focuses on social skills necessary for co-creation and teamwork. This includes fostering trust, a shared sense of purpose, and a culture of inclusivity.

5. Acting: Involves the practical application of these skills, particularly in leadership and action-taking. It includes courage, and determination, , enabling people to take decisive actions toward the SDGs.

The IDGs offer tools for leaders, educators, and organisations to develop these inner capabilities we need for the personal transformation that connects us to global change.

This transformation is not just crucial—it is our path forward, beyond the limitations of technophilia and toward the genuine cooperation that will save our planet.

WHAT CAN WE DO BY FRIDAY?

The DeGrowth Master.

Me: I'm so excited I'm about to buy a new car.

The DeGrowth Master: Why do you want to buy a new car?

Me: Because this one I found is fancy. I love its new dash-spanning digital display, level 3 automated driving, and adaptive air suspensions. My current car doesn't have them.

The DeGrowth Master: Why do you want dash-spanning digital display?

Me: Because it makes me feel like a modern man well-equipped with the latest gizmo. I love that.

The DeGrowth Master: Let me ask you this. Why do you need to feel like a modern man?

Me (getting annoyed): Mind your own business.

The DeGrowth Master: Did you read Professor Kohei Saito's latest book?

Me: Yes. I mean, no I did not. When I went online to read the book reviews the website displayed giant advertising banners featuring second-hand jackets from my favourite Italian designer. I bought two jackets.

The DeGrowth Master: Why did you buy two jackets?

Me (Clueless): Why not? It's cheap and second-hand, totally worth it.

The DeGrowth Master: I was talking to you about Professor Kohei Saito's latest book. Are you interested in hearing more?

Me: A b s o l u t e l y. I told you I tried to read the reviews. What is it all about?

The DeGrowth Master: The book is called "Slow Down: The Degrowth Manifesto". Is that talking to you?

Me: Nah. It doesn't. I get the gist, but I'm past the Degrowth idea. I love buying stuff. It makes me feel good. And I consume in a responsible way. My car is electric. My jackets are second-hand. And I systematically offset my flights' carbon emissions.

The DeGrowth Master: I got it. You're attached to your privileged same-day delivery consumerist lifestyle. Can I now tell you a bit more about Professor Saito's work?

Me: Indulge yourself

The DeGrowth Master: Professor Saito explains that Green Capitalism, what you've been promoting with great passion throughout much of your career, is a fallacy,

Me: I don't believe it. Go Green Tech. Solar panels everywhere, recycled biomaterials and hydrogen powered flying cars that get me from Manhattan to JFK in 15 minutes. That's what I want. And low-carbon aluminium from zero-emissions steelmaking from New Zealand, so my Apple watch can be carbon neutral.

By the way, did you see the latest carbon-neutral Apple watch advertising? Mother Nature comes as a bossy board member who interviews Tim Cook and his team. Apple is smashing it. By 2030, all Apple products will have a net-zero climate impact.

The DeGrowth Master: Hold your horses.

Me: But Tim said it

The DeGrowth Master: Can you slow down?

Me: Sure. Go ahead.

The DeGrowth Master: Do you know about the Netherlands' Fallacy?

Me: No. Never been there. But I definitely want to,

The DeGrowth Master: Glad to know. The Netherlands' Fallacy speaks about the country's illusory attainment of both high-level standards and low levels of pollution. It is only achieved by displacing externalities. This means by pushing the degradation of environmental resources to other countries, those acting as manufacturing facilities for the Netherlands. That's what Professor Saito explains in his book. He argues that if we are serious about the climate crisis, we must abandon the growth obsession and the GDP mantra because we won't be saved by electric cars.

Me: Bullshit. I love my electric car.

The DeGrowth Master: We know that. Marx too, thought, at least initially, that innovation would raise living standards. That's what the book exposes. Marx later on realised that in fact, all Capitalism was doing was displacing the toll on labourers and the cost of pollution on others, like what's happening during the extraction of the rare minerals used in your fancy Electric car battery.

Me: It can't be worse than burning fossil fuel. And we're coming up with new methods of extraction that minimise mining's environmental impact. Look, I can't go Marx or International Communist. I understand the Doughnuts economy, I want to work toward all of this. But I'm also realistic about where we're at and the forces we need to shift.

The DeGrowth Master: You sound like someone looking for excuses not to face the reality of the crisis. Think about what's happening in China, Africa, and India, where standards of living are increasing exponentially. Think about the gigantic quantity of resources we need to feed this augmentation in global consumption.

Me: I am. What do you suggest?

The DeGrowth Master: I suggest we live within our planetary boundaries.

Me: Which means?

The DeGrowth Master: It means recognizing the finite nature of the Earth's resources and the critical ecological thresholds we must respect to avoid pushing our planet beyond its capacity. The work of scientists like Johan Rockström and the Stockholm Resilience Centre has outlined nine such planetary boundaries—safe limits for things like climate stability, biodiversity, land use, ocean acidification, the nitrogen cycle and others. We've already crossed the limits of several of them, yet we continue to expand our consumption and polluting manufacturing.

Me: So, do I need to stop buying new things?

The DeGrowth Master: Not necessarily, but we should rethink our unbridled use of resources. We must shift from increasing material wealth to re-engineering our financial and regulatory systems to recognise the true impact of our actions and decisions.

Me: And how does that connect to my electric car or those jackets?

The DeGrowth Master: It's not about rejecting technology or second-hand fashion. It's about taking responsibility for the broader impacts of our choices. Electric cars and second-hand goods are good, but they still require resources and energy, and they still come with environmental costs.

Me: Alright, you're pushing for a profound shift in the very systems that govern our societies, don't you?

The DeGrowth Master: I am. And that's a new model of prosperity—one that values sustainability, community, and planetary health over blind expansion. And that works for future generations.

Me: I do like that. Now what's next for my new car?

The DeGrowth Master: As for your new car… how about a weekend rental instead? Do you know about Turo? Shared rentals let you enjoy that fancy car without the long-term environmental toll.

Me: Turo, huh? So I can still drive a fancy car, but just rent it when I need it?

The DeGrowth Master: Exactly. It's about shifting from ownership to access. Enjoy the perks without fuelling the endless cycle of production, consumption, and waste. Plus, you're making the most of shared resources.

Me: Not bad. So I can have the modern tech without the guilt.

The DeGrowth Master: That's the idea. Go enjoy it. But remember—it's about smart choices, not more stuff.

What would Roger do?

It's been years of hearing them weep and lament.

Work is tough. They can't break through.

The CEO missed their meeting, the CFO rejected their proposal.

In the litany of corporate programs, they leave the battlefield scarred.

Who are they?

The Sustainability Managers. A passionate, peculiar breed of experts.

They might be the Head of ESG for an Asset Manager, the Climate Lead of a Farm Cooperative, or the Chief Sustainability Officer of a mass retail group. The businesses they work for are key players in the global economy.

These new experts are tasked with designing what's often dubbed the Net Zero Plan—the plan to transform their organisation from a clueless polluter—or worse, a perpetrator—to a lead actor engaged in the climate transition of the world economy.

What for?

For the grand slam. The Spirito Santo.

To transform into organisations that actively contribute to avoiding the worst effects of Climate Change - without losing sight of their commercial mandate.

Sustainability Managers understand the law of gravity, which states that the love of money trumps the love of our planet.

Yet, as Sisyphus, they carry the weight of humanity on their shoulders. Relentless, they keep mewling at the door of the powerful.

Let's change the scene.

On May 6, 1954, at Oxford's Iffley Road track, Roger Bannister completed the mile in 3 minutes 59.4 seconds. At that time, the sub-four-minute mile was considered beyond the limits of human capability, almost as the "law of gravity".

Bannister's achievement altered the mindset in athletics. There was a "before Bannister" and an "after".

Bannister proved that the right training, strategy, and mental preparation could overcome perceived physical barriers.

Once Bannister broke the 4-minute barrier, just 46 days later, Australian runner John Landy ran the mile in 3 minutes 57.9 seconds.

Athletes waited for 104 years - since early 1850 with the first official timed mile race -. to break the four-minute mile. Once it was broken once, it was broken again and again and again.

Anytime I hear a Sustainability Manager weep, I keep going back to Roger Bannister four-minute mile. What would Roger do?

A breakthrough in one company's Net Zero Plan could set off a chain reaction across the industry, much like Bannister's accomplishments in athletics.

Imagine if the CFO of a major food retailer or bank not only approved a Net Zero Plan but championed it. How rapidly would entire parts of the economy turnaround from climate laggards to climate leaders?

It's not all bleak out there. There are real-life "Roger Bannisters" in business, proving that sustainability and commercial success can go hand in hand.

Larry Fink at BlackRock shook up the financial world by telling CEOs that ignoring climate risks was no option. (Yes, you are correct, he subsequently adjusted his position to address the weaponisation of ESG in the US).

Steven van Rijswijk at ING says to get serious about climate action or lose funding from the bank.

And then there's Paul Polman, who fundamentally transformed Unilever into a model of sustainable growth, proving that businesses can thrive while protecting the planet.

These leaders are showing the world that breaking through corporate inertia is possible. They're the Roger Bannisters of climate action, challenging the old rules and setting a new pace for the future.

What Can we do by Friday?

Unleash the Roger Bannister in you.

The right combination of unique regimens includes finding unexpected allies in the company, using data to make an irrefutable case, identifying pre-stage technologies that can alter the emissions profile, or starting small pilot projects that showcase what's possible.

Train, practice, and break the law of gravity.

The Planet will love you for it.

Sweeping Changes.

Sweeping changes are bold actions that fundamentally alter the course of history.

In 1893, New Zealand passed the Electoral Act, granting women the right to vote. This sparked women's suffrage movements worldwide. That qualifies as a sweeping change.

In 1964, the United States passed the Civil Rights Act, outlawing discrimination based on race, colour, religion, sex, or national origin. A sweeping change.

In 1987, the US and other nations spearheaded the Montreal Protocol, phasing out ozone-depleting CFCs. It remains one of the most successful environmental agreements in history. Another sweeping change.

In 2000, Iceland introduced a parental leave law that provided equal leave for both parents. This reshaped family dynamics inspiring similar policies worldwide. A sweeping change.

In 2002, Bangladesh banned single-use plastic bags, recognising their devastating impact on the environment. A sweeping change.

In 2003, London introduced a £15.00 daily congestion charge to reduce vehicle emissions and improve air quality. This is a sweeping change.

In 2023, France banned short-haul flights, sending a powerful message as a world first. Though limited to three routes, it was still a sweeping change.

In 2025, New Zealand requires publicly listed companies to disclose their climate-related risks and their scope 3 emissions, allowing investors to assess the full scope of these risks. A sweeping change.

Sweeping changes are bold, game-changing, fact-based actions that transform societal outcomes.

What sweeping change will you create?

Everything Tastes Better in Paris.

In 2023, tobacco-related diseases caused over 8 million deaths globally.

Yet, you can still buy a pack of cigarettes for 6 Euros in Madrid or 12 Euros in Paris. Same toxins, pricier in Paris because, well, it's Paris.

Philip Morris International, the multinational behind Marlboro, aims for a smoke-free portfolio by 2030.

Each year, air pollution is responsible for an estimated 7 million premature deaths worldwide, with a significant portion linked to the burning of fossil fuels.

BP calls itself *Beyond Petroleum*, and TotalEnergies brands itself as *the company of all energie*s.

But what if these companies truly meant it? What if they stood up and said, *"Not one more life should be lost because of our products"?"* They would see the transition from their legacy businesses not as a burden, but as the greatest investment in their legacy, and in humanity's future.

Yet, we continue living in a world of compromises. Business leaders delay sustainability investments, while others keep smoking.

There's no neat conclusion to that story, just the complexity of human nature and the opportunities we miss. Our illogical selves that ignore the obvious, even when life is at stake.

What can you do by Friday?

It should be obvious.

Nature Bats Last.

Yvon Chouinard.

Let My People Go Surfing

How Sustainable Are You?

Question:	Never 0	Rarely 1	Sometimes 2	Often 3	Always 4
When I fly, I offset my carbon emissions.					
I recycle or compost household waste.					
I choose public transport, bike, or carpool to reduce my carbon footprint.					
When shopping, I prioritise products made from sustainable or recycled materials.					
I turn the lights off when I leave the room.					
I grow some of the food I eat.					
I limit my use of single-use plastics (e.g. bags, straws, packaging) beyond what is regulated.					
I purchase second-hand, refurbished, or upcycled products instead of new.					
I drink tap water at restaurants.					

Question:	Never	Rarely	Sometimes	Often	Always
	0	1	2	3	4
I get seriously pis*ed off when other people make poor sustainability choices.					
I actively reduce my red meat and dairy consumption.					
I often repair items instead of throwing them away.					
I get involved in community environmental action (e.g., volunteering, advocacy).					
I keep myself up to date on environmental issues and sustainable practices.					
I intentionally minimize my clothing purchases. (i.e. "Buy once and buy well" versus impulse buying).					
I seek out and use energy from renewable sources.					
I store and eat my leftover food?					
I choose brands that are transparent about their environmental practices.					
I drive an EV.					
I jump at the chance to participate in sustainable practices at my workplace.					

Question:	Never	Rarely	Sometimes	Often	Always
	0	1	2	3	4
I am happy to have a "zoom" meeting rather than fly to be in the room.					
I volunteer in community activities focused on environmental sustainability.					
I know my organization prioritises sustainable sourcing, production, or operational practices.					
I am very proud of the efforts my organization is making to encourage sustainability.					
When I vote, a candidate's environmental policies play an important role in my choice.					
Total:					

Add your scores from the previous page (0 for never; 1 for rarely… etc) and find your persona below.

Score	Persona	Summary	Common Traits
0-20	The Indifferent Bystander	This individual shows almost no interest in sustainability and makes little to no	*Detached, passive, unmotivated*

		effort to engage with it. Some may be actively "anti-green" They are at best passive, with convenience or ignorance driving their choices. Sustainability is not on their radar.	
21-40	The Unconvinced Consumer	The Unconvinced Consumer takes small steps when it's convenient but remains inconsistent. They are aware of the importance of sustainability in a general sense, but have not yet made it a priority in their daily life. Their actions are often well-meaning but selective.	*Aware, conservative, tentative.*
41-60	The Emerging Steward	This person is actively making changes and becoming more engaged with sustainability. They try to live consciously and are aware of the environmental	*Evolving, intentional, learning.*

		impact of their choices. They are still working to integrate sustainability more fully into their lifestyle, but they want to, and are, making progress.	
61-80	The Dedicated Practitioner	For the Dedicated Practitioner, sustainability drives a lot of their decisions. They consistently make choices that reduce their environmental impact, and they have incorporated sustainable practices into most areas of their life. They are proactive and often take leadership in sustainability efforts at home, work, or in their community. They may still struggle to take big "difficult" sustainability decisions.	*Committed, deliberate, resourceful.*

81-100	The Relentless Warrior	Sustainability is the core of the Relentless Advocate's life. They take bold and sometimes difficult actions to reduce their environmental footprint and actively push for systemic change. They are passionate and often lead by example in their community or organization.	*Driven, uncompromising, leadership-oriented.*

Does that sound like you?

What areas could you improve your score by Friday?

Can you get to the next level in the next 3 months?

12 Months, 12 Corporate Climate Actions

January: Materiality Assessment

Start the year by getting real. Is your business leading, following, or lagging in sustainability and climate action? What impact does it have on the world around you, and how is the world around you impacting your business's ability to succeed?

Find out by conducting a materiality assessment. This process helps you identify which issues matter most to your business and your key stakeholders. It will help you decide where to focus your efforts. It will also help you prioritise initiatives to adapt your business to the most practical aspects of climate change, circularity, diversity and inclusion, education, and other societal forces shaping the future of business. January resolutions first.

February: Set Science-Based Targets

Climate change isn't a guessing game—it's science. The Intergovernmental Panel on Climate Change (IPCC) defines how much carbon can be released into the atmosphere based on the goal of keeping global warming below 1.5°C to 2°C. Your company's emissions targets need to align with what the planet can handle, not just what looks good on paper.

Set science-based targets (SBTi). These targets ensure that your business is on track to reduce emissions in line with global climate goals. It's not just about looking green—it's about making sure your business survives and thrives in a low-carbon future.

March: Internal Carbon Tax

Every ton your company emits has a cost—whether it's to the environment, your reputation, or your bottom line. By assigning an internal price to carbon, you make everyone in your company feel the impact of their decisions on emissions. Suddenly, that business flight doesn't seem so essential, and those energy-intensive processes start looking a little less attractive.

Whether you use a shadow price (for internal decision-making) or a carbon fee (charging departments based on their emissions), you're putting a value on what's often treated as invisible.

The result? Carbon-conscious choices at every level of the business. And it's not just a feel-good move—it gets your company ahead of the curve as carbon taxes and regulations tighten globally.

April: EV Month

Time to ditch the gas-guzzlers. Those petro cars aren't just bad for the planet—they're draining your budget too. Electric vehicles (EVs) are cleaner, safer, and could cost your business less if financed appropriately. And if you want to level up, install EV charging stations on-site. Your employees (and the planet) will thank you.

May: Products Lifecycle Assessment

How green are your products, really? Are they full-on green, a little grey, or a lot brown? Time to find out. A lifecycle assessment (LCA) measures the environmental impact of a product from raw material sourcing to disposal. Conduct a full LCA and see where you're making the biggest impact—and where you need to improve. This will also help you share all the good news with your customers and investors, especially those for whom greener is better.

June: Capabilities Building

Get your employees fired up. Sustainability isn't just your problem (or your opportunity). You'll need capabilities across your organisation—in operations, finance, supply chain, sourcing, and procurement—to make real progress. So empower your team members by launching a dedicated, organisation-wide training program. Host a climate innovation day. Offer prizes for the best ideas—those that green your value chain and also save money or grow revenue. Climate action is a long-term game, not a three-day race.

July: Climate-Proof Your Finances

Have you factored climate risks into your financial planning? If not, it's time. But what does that mean? It's about ensuring your company is prepared for the financial impacts of climate change—whether it's rising energy costs, disrupted supply chains, or extreme weather events damaging assets. Assess how these risks could affect your bottom line and build them into your budgets, forecasts, and investment decisions.

- **If you're a real estate company**, more frequent floods could impact the value of your properties. You need to factor in location risks and invest in climate-resilient infrastructure.

- **If you're a dairy farm**, extreme weather can affect livestock and crop yields, disrupting your supply and increasing costs. Plan for climate-related fluctuations in production.

- **If you're an insurance business**, you're likely facing higher claims due to severe weather events. Adjust your policies and premiums to account for increased risk exposure.

In fact, whichever sector you work in, climate is now part of financial planning. Get your CFO grooving.

August: Switch to 100% Renewable Energy

Still using fossil fuels? Why? Get on the phone with your energy provider, or start installing solar panels. In fact, you don't even have to get on the roof—virtual rooftop solar solutions are now available in most countries. Switching to 100% renewable energy will reduce your energy costs and shield your company from future carbon taxes or regulations. It's also a great selling point for customers and investors.

Whether it's solar, wind, or geothermal, the options are now easy to access. And don't forget, many governments offer incentives and tax breaks for renewable energy investments. That's when the penny drops.

September: Close the Recycling Loop

Start a circular economy program and find ways to keep your products and materials in use instead of sending them to the landfill. That's a biggie. It can drive customer loyalty and spark product innovation. But that biggie ain't easy. It takes creativity and astuteness to move from the linear "buy-use-discard" model to a place where processing and reusing materials becomes attractive and affordable.

Yes, those Prada Re-Nylon jackets made from 100% recycled nylon look cool. But what we're talking about is broader, bigger, and more complex. It's about creating logistics, technology, and finance systems that keep goods "in the loop" at an everyday, affordable cost. Today, we've barely scratched the surface of the opportunity.

One example I love? Royal Auping, a Dutch bed manufacturer, uses circular design principles to create mattresses that can be easily disassembled and recycled. Or Critical, a Māori-owned business in New Zealand, is building both the products and the technology platform to transform plastic waste into beautiful, low-carbon, and endlessly recyclable material.

They've done it. You can do it, too.

October: Offset What You Can't Cut

Can't eliminate all your emissions to Zero? No problem. Buy some carbon offsets to cover the rest while you develop the capacities and insights to get to zero. Look for credible offset programs that meet the strictest global standards. Offsets can't be a shortcut—they're a temporary way to deal with the emissions you genuinely can't reduce yet. In the race to carbon-neutral, every ton of CO_2 matters.

November: Partner for Impact

Climate action doesn't happen in isolation. Find a partner or join a sustainability alliance to scale up your efforts and make a bigger dent. There powerful platforms out there that can help you connect and collaborate.

Start with the World Business Council for Sustainable Development (WBCSD), which brings companies together to tackle sustainability challenges. Or look to organizations like WWF and Conservation International, which offer partnerships focused on ethical sourcing and environmental protection. For supply chain transparency and ethical practices, platforms like the Ellen MacArthur Foundation and the Sustainable Apparel Coalition are worth exploring.

Big challenges need big solutions, and working together is the best way to tackle the climate crisis.

December: Publish a Sustainability Report

Tell the world what you're up to.

Publish your sustainability progress, even if you're still figuring things out. People love transparency. But please, make your report short, about targets, data, and progress. We don't need a flurry of pretty pictures. We need the real story—what's working, what's not, where you've scored, and where you've missed the mark.

Look to the Global Reporting Initiative (GRI), CDP (Carbon Disclosure Project), and SASB (Sustainability Accounting Standards Board) for frameworks that can guide your reporting. These organizations set the gold standard in transparent, data-driven sustainability reports.

Some of the best examples? Nike, Patagonia, and Unilever are leading the way in sustainability reporting. They show the good, the bad, and the real, without sugarcoating.

Follow their lead, and you'll build trust with your stakeholders and customers.

Te toto o te tangata, kai, te oranga o te tangata, he whenua.

While food provides the blood in our veins, our health is drawn from the land.

Māori Whakatauki (Proverb)

Section 5.

Resources

The world leading sustainability organisations.

World Business Council for Sustainable Development (WBCSD):
https://www.wbcsd.org

WWF (World Wildlife Fund):
https://www.worldwildlife.org

Conservation International:
https://www.conservation.org

Ellen MacArthur Foundation:
https://www.ellenmacarthurfoundation.org

Sustainable Apparel Coalition:
https://apparelcoalition.org

Global Reporting Initiative (GRI) Database:
https://database.globalreporting.org/

Science Based Target initiative:

https://sciencebasedtargets.org/

CDP (Carbon Disclosure Project) A-List Companies:
https://www.cdp.net/en/companies/companies-scores

SASB (Sustainability Accounting Standards Board) Case Studies:
https://www.sasb.org/case-studies/

Corporate Register Reporting Awards (CRRA):
http://www.corporateregister.com/crra/

52 key Sustainability terms.

Here are 52 key terms to include in your climate action lexicon:

1. **Biodiversity:** The variety of plant and animal life in the world or in a particular habitat, crucial for ecosystem health and resilience.

2. **Blue Economy:** The sustainable use of ocean resources for economic growth, improved livelihoods, and jobs, while preserving the health of ocean ecosystems.

3. **Carbon Border Adjustment Mechanism (CBAM):** A policy tool to apply a carbon price on imported goods to prevent carbon leakage.

4. **Carbon Budget:** The maximum amount of carbon dioxide emissions permitted over a period of time to keep within a certain temperature threshold.

5. **Carbon Capture and Storage (CCS):** A technology to capture and store carbon dioxide emissions from sources like power plants and industrial facilities.

6. **Carbon Footprint:** The total amount of greenhouse gases emitted directly or indirectly by an individual, organization, event, or product.

7. **Carbon Intensity:** The amount of carbon (in CO2 emissions) released per unit of another variable such as energy produced, GDP, or population.

8. **Carbon Leakage:** The situation that occurs when companies transfer production to other countries with

looser environmental regulations, leading to no reduction in overall emissions.

9. **Carbon Neutral:** Achieving net-zero carbon emissions by balancing emitted carbon with an equivalent amount offset or removed.

10. **Carbon Offset:** A reduction in emissions of carbon dioxide or other greenhouse gases made in order to compensate for emissions made elsewhere.

11. **Carbon Pricing:** A cost applied to carbon pollution to encourage polluters to reduce the amount of greenhouse gases they emit.

12. **Carbon Sequestration:** The process of capturing and storing atmospheric carbon dioxide in order to mitigate or defer global warming.

13. **Carbon Tax:** A fee imposed on the burning of carbon-based fuels intended to reduce greenhouse gas emissions.

14. **Circular Economy:** An economic system aimed at eliminating waste and the continual use of resources through reuse, recycling, and remanufacturing.

15. **Climate Action Plan:** A comprehensive strategy outlining steps to mitigate and adapt to climate change impacts.

16. **Climate Adaptation:** Adjusting practices, processes, and structures to reduce the harm or take advantage of opportunities associated with climate change.

17. **Climate Justice:** A term that captures the equity aspects of climate change, considering its effects on the most vulnerable populations.

18. **Climate Positive:** Going beyond achieving net-zero carbon emissions to create an environmental benefit by removing additional carbon dioxide from the atmosphere.

19. **Climate Resilience:** The ability to anticipate, prepare for, and respond to hazardous events or disturbances related to climate change.

20. **Corporate Social Responsibility (CSR):** A self-regulating business model that helps a company be socially accountable to itself, its stakeholders, and the public.

21. **Decarbonization:** The process of reducing carbon emissions associated with electricity, transport, heating, and industrial production.

22. **Emission Trading System (ETS):** A market-based approach used to control pollution by providing economic incentives for reducing the emissions of pollutants.

23. **Energy Efficiency:** Using less energy to perform the same task, reducing energy waste.

24. **Environmental Footprint:** The impact of human activities measured in terms of the amount of resources consumed and waste produced.

25. **Environmental Impact Assessment (EIA):** A process of evaluating the likely environmental impacts of a proposed project or development, taking into account interrelated socio-economic, cultural, and human-health impacts.

26. **Environmental Management System (EMS):** A framework that helps an organization achieve its environmental goals through consistent review, evaluation, and improvement of its environmental performance.

27. **Environmental Policy:** Statements and guidelines provided by an organization outlining its intentions and principles regarding its environmental performance.

28. **Environmental Stewardship:** The responsible use and protection of the natural environment through conservation and sustainable practices.

29. **Environmental, Social, and Governance (ESG) Reporting:** Disclosing a company's impact in these three key areas to stakeholders and investors.

30. **ESG (Environmental, Social, and Governance):** A set of criteria used to evaluate a company's impact from an environmental, social and governance perspective.

31. **Green Bonds:** Bonds specifically earmarked to be used for climate and environmental projects.

32. **Green Building:** The practice of creating structures using processes and materials that are environmentally responsible and resource-efficient throughout a building's life cycle.

33. **Green Consumerism:** A form of consumer activism that is based on the concept of buying in priority products that are environmentally friendly and generally carrty

34. **Green Economy:** An economy that aims at reducing environmental risks and ecological scarcities while

increasing sustainable development without degrading the environment.

35. **Green Finance:** Financing investments that provide environmental benefits in the broader context of sustainable development.

36. **Green Infrastructure:** A network providing the "ingredients" for solving urban and climatic challenges by building with nature.

37. **Green Procurement:** The process of purchasing products and services that have a reduced environmental impact.

38. **Green Supply Chain Management:** Integrating sustainable environmental processes into the traditional supply chain.

39. **Greenhouse Gases (GHGs):** Gases that trap heat in the atmosphere, contributing to the greenhouse effect and climate change. Common GHGs include carbon dioxide, methane, and nitrous oxide.

40. **Greenwashing:** Misleading information disseminated by an organization to present an environmentally responsible public image.

41. **Life Cycle Assessment (LCA):** A technique to assess the environmental aspects and potential impacts associated with a product, process, or service.

42. **Nature-Based Solutions (NBS):** Actions that protect, sustainably manage, and restore natural or modified ecosystems to address societal challenges effectively and adaptively, providing human well-being and biodiversity benefits.

43. **Net Zero:** The balance between the amount of greenhouse gas produced and the amount removed from the atmosphere.

44. **Paris Agreement:** An international treaty adopted in 2015 to limit global warming to below 2 degrees Celsius compared to pre-industrial levels.

45. **Renewable Energy:** Energy from naturally replenished sources such as wind, solar, hydropower, geothermal, or tidal. Nuclear energy is generally considered a source of renewable energy.

46. **Renewable Energy Certificates (RECs):** Tradable certificates that represent proof that one megawatt-hour of electricity was generated from an eligible renewable energy resource.

47. **SBT (Science-Based Targets):** Climate targets aligned with what the latest climate science says is necessary to meet the goals of the Paris Agreement.

48. **Scope 1, 2, and 3 Emissions:**

    o **Scope 1:** Direct emissions from owned or controlled sources.

    o **Scope 2:** Indirect emissions from the generation of purchased electricity, steam, heating, and cooling consumed by the reporting company.

    o **Scope 3:** All other indirect emissions that occur in a company's value chain.

49. **Sustainable Business Model:** A business model that integrates economic, social, and environmental factors into its operations and decision-making processes.

50. **Sustainable Development Goals (SDGs):** A collection of 17 global goals set by the United Nations General Assembly in 2015 for the year 2030, aimed at achieving a better and more sustainable future for all.

51. **Sustainability:** Meeting the needs of the present without compromising the ability of future generations to meet their own needs.

52. **Zero Waste:** A philosophy that encourages redesign so that all products are reused, and no trash is sent to landfills or incinerators.

The ten books that have defined sustainability.

Silent Spring by Rachel Carson (1962)

Silent Spring is credited with igniting the modern environmental movement. Rachel Carson meticulously documented the harmful effects of pesticides, particularly DDT, on wildlife, particularly birds. The book raised public awareness about the dangers of chemical pollution and led to the eventual ban of DDT in many countries. It remains a foundational text in environmentalism.

Limits to Growth by Donella Meadows, Dennis Meadows, Jørgen Randes, and William Behrens (1972)

This pioneering report, commissioned by the Club of Rome, used computer modelling to forecast the long-term impact of unchecked population and economic growth on Earth's finite resources. It presented alarming predictions about resource depletion, environmental degradation, and the unsustainable path of industrialization. Though controversial at the time, the book has proven prescient in its warning about the environmental and economic crises we face today. Its call for sustainable growth still resonates in discussions about the future of humanity.

The Triple Bottom Line: Rebuilding Business and Creating Value with Sustainability by John Elkington (1997)

John Elkington's *The Triple Bottom Line* introduces the concept of sustainability through a framework that measures business success based on three key pillars: people, planet, and profit. Elkington argues that companies should focus not only on financial outcomes but also on their social and environmental impact. He advocates for a shift in how businesses operate, urging them to embrace long-term value creation through sustainable practices. The book has been pivotal in reshaping corporate responsibility and encouraging businesses to incorporate sustainability into their core strategies.

Natural Capitalism: Creating the Next Industrial Revolution by Paul Hawken, Amory Lovins, and L. Hunter Lovins (1999)

Natural Capitalism offers a revolutionary approach to how businesses can align with ecological sustainability. The authors argue that economic systems have historically ignored natural capital—earth's ecosystems and biodiversity—and propose innovative business models that value efficiency, renewable resources, and reduced waste. The book is filled with practical examples of how industries can redesign their processes to benefit both the environment and profitability. It promotes the idea of working with nature, not against it, to achieve lasting economic and environmental health.

Cradle to Cradle: Remaking the Way We Make Things by William McDonough and Michael Braungart (2002)

Cradle to Cradle advocates for an entirely new design philosophy, where products are created with their eventual reuse in mind, eliminating the concept of waste. McDonough and Braungart envision a circular economy where materials constantly flow through closed-loop systems, mimicking natural ecosystems. Instead of "cradle to grave" (where products end in landfills), their approach ensures that everything created can be reused, repurposed, or biodegraded. This book has been highly influential in design, architecture, and product manufacturing, pushing for eco-effectiveness rather than mere eco-efficiency.

Braiding Sweetgrass: Indigenous Wisdom, Scientific Knowledge, and the Teachings of Plants by Robin Wall Kimmerer (2013)

Robin Wall Kimmerer, a botanist and member of the Citizen Potawatomi Nation, weaves together indigenous wisdom and scientific knowledge to illustrate how humans can live in reciprocity with nature. Through personal stories and plant ecology, Kimmerer explores the importance of gratitude, humility, and respect for the natural world. She offers a vision of sustainability rooted in mutual care between people and the environment, blending ecological science with spiritual traditions. *Braiding Sweetgrass* resonates deeply with those seeking a more profound connection to the earth.

Drawdown: The Most Comprehensive Plan Ever Proposed to Reverse Global Warming edited by Paul Hawken (2017)

Drawdown presents a detailed, science-backed collection of the most effective solutions for reversing global warming, using existing technologies and methods. Compiled by experts, the book outlines 100 solutions ranging from renewable energy and electric vehicles to regenerative agriculture and better building practices. Each solution is ranked by its potential impact, cost, and timeline to draw down atmospheric carbon. *Drawdown* is an optimistic, action-oriented guide that emphasizes the possibility of mitigating climate change if these solutions are scaled and implemented widely.

The Uninhabitable Earth: Life After Warming David Wallace-Wells (2019)

David Wallace-Wells paints a chilling picture of a future transformed by climate change in *The Uninhabitable Earth*. He explores the terrifying consequences of inaction—rising sea levels, extreme heat, food shortages, and climate-driven conflicts. The book highlights how these disasters are already underway and will only worsen if the world fails to act swiftly. While apocalyptic in tone, Wallace-Wells uses his narrative to press the urgency of addressing climate change before it leads to irreversible damage

The Ministry for the Future. Kim Stanley Robinson (2020)

The Ministry for the Future is a speculative fiction novel that takes place in the near future, where climate disasters have escalated to unbearable levels. The novel follows an international agency designed to advocate for future generations and the planet itself, experimenting with various geoengineering and policy solutions. Kim Stanley Robinson mixes dramatic storytelling with real-world science and policy debates, making the book both entertaining and thought-provoking. It's a hopeful, albeit realistic, look at the challenges and potential solutions to the climate crisis.

Net Positive: How Courageous Companies Thrive by Giving More Than They Take by Paul Polman and Andrew Winston (2021)

Net Positive offers a blueprint for how businesses can move beyond sustainability and contribute positively to society and the environment. Paul Polman, former CEO of Unilever, and co-author Andrew Winston argue that companies must not only minimize their negative impacts but also create value that benefits all stakeholders, including the planet. The book outlines real-world examples of companies leading with purpose and demonstrates how this approach can drive long-term business success. It is an essential read for corporate leaders aiming to integrate sustainability into their core strategies.

The pioneers of Sustainable Business.

These are the sustainability pioneers we have been learning from.

They have shaped the sustainability movement in their respective fields, from environmental advocacy and business innovation to fashion, food, and energy. In addition to business leaders, we have included key scientists and one activist we have been following with great interest.

Al Gore

Gore, former Vice President of the United States, became a leading environmental advocate through his 2006 documentary An Inconvenient Truth. In 2007, he was awarded the Nobel Peace Prize for his work in climate advocacy. He is also a partner at Generation Investment Management, a firm that focuses on sustainable investing and has been instrumental in integrating environmental, social, and governance factors into financial markets.

Amory Lovins

Lovins, co-founder of the Rocky Mountain Institute, has been a pioneer in promoting energy efficiency and renewable energy solutions. His work, including numerous books and reports (notably Natural Capitalism in 1999), has influenced the development of sustainable design and energy systems. Amory Lovins' wife is Hunter Lovins, an

American environmentalist, author, and social entrepreneur, co-founder of Natural Capitalism Solutions.

Anita Roddick

Roddick was the founder of The Body Shop, which she established in 1976 with a focus on ethical sourcing and environmental sustainability. Her commitment to activism and fair trade set new standards in corporate responsibility and social entrepreneurship.

Dan Barber

Barber, a chef and advocate for sustainable food systems, has used his restaurants and initiatives to promote regenerative agriculture, local sourcing, and crop diversity. His 2009 work The Third Plate explores the future of food sustainability.

David Attenborough

Attenborough, a naturalist and broadcaster, has been a tireless advocate for conservation and sustainability. His documentaries, including The Blue Planet (2001) and Our Planet (2019), have raised global awareness about the environmental crisis and the importance of biodiversity.

Emmanuel Faber

Faber is the former CEO **of** Danone, a global leader in the food and beverage industry. Under his leadership,

Danone embraced a commitment to environmental goals, such as reducing carbon emissions and improving water usage. Faber has been a vocal advocate for the need to incorporate sustainability into corporate governance and business strategy, and he has been instrumental in driving corporate responsibility in the global food sector.

E.O. Wilson

Wilson, a biologist and naturalist, has had a profound impact on biodiversity and conservation. His work, including his 1992 book The Diversity of Life, has influenced global environmental policies and conservation efforts.

James Lovelock

Lovelock is a scientist known for formulating the Gaia theory in 1979, which suggests that Earth and its ecosystems function as a single, self-regulating entity. His work has reshaped our understanding of environmental change and global ecological balance.

John Elkington

Elkington, a pioneer in sustainability, coined the term "Triple Bottom Line" in 1994, emphasizing the balance of social, environmental, and economic factors in business practices. His work has influenced the integration of sustainability into corporate strategy worldwide.

Mary Robinson

Robinson, the first female President of Ireland (1990–1997), has been an advocate for climate justice, focusing on the intersection of human rights and climate change. In 2009, she founded the Mary Robinson Foundation – Climate Justice, which works to promote a fair and equitable response to climate change.

Mark Carney

Carney, former Governor of the Bank of Canada and the Bank of England, is a prominent advocate for integrating climate risk into financial decision-making. As the UN Special Envoy for Climate Action and Finance, Carney has worked to mobilize the financial sector towards aligning investments with climate goals.

Michael Bloomberg

Bloomberg, the founder of Bloomberg LP and former mayor of New York City, has been a key figure in advancing sustainability in finance. His company's data and analytics services have helped businesses and governments integrate environmental, social, and governance (ESG) criteria into investment decisions. He has also launched the **C40 Cities Climate Leadership Group**, which focuses on reducing emissions and addressing climate change in major cities around the world.

Paul Polman

Polman, former CEO of Unilever (2009–2019), was a key advocate for integrating sustainability into business practices. He led Unilever's efforts to reduce environmental impact, promote fair trade, and adopt long-term sustainable business models. In 2010, he introduced the Unilever Sustainable Living Plan.

Ray Anderson

Anderson, ex CEO of Interface, became famous for transforming the carpet company into a sustainability leader after what he called his "spear in the chest" moment in 1994, when he read Paul Hawken's "The Ecology of Commerce" and completely changed the company's environmental approach. He set ambitious sustainability goals with his "Mission Zero" initiative, aiming to eliminate any negative impact Interface had on the environment by 2020.

Stella McCartney

McCartney, the famed daughter of Paul McCartney, has been a leader in promoting sustainable fashion. Since the 2000s, she has used organic and cruelty-free materials in her collections and has advocated for reducing the environmental footprint of the fashion industry.

Yvon Chouinard

Chouinard is the founder of Patagonia, a company that has led the way in environmental responsibility. Since its founding in 1973, Patagonia has focused on sustainable materials, ethical manufacturing practices, and environmental advocacy, becoming a leader in corporate sustainability.

Vanessa Nakate

Nakate, a Ugandan climate activist, has been a powerful advocate for climate justice, particularly in Africa. She founded the Rise Up Movement and has been an outspoken voice at international climate conferences, calling for greater inclusion of African voices in the global climate conversation and highlighting the disproportionate impact of climate change on vulnerable communities.

www.ingramcontent.com/pod-product-compliance
Lightning Source LLC
Chambersburg PA
CBHW041644310326
41914CB00129BA/2065/J

Thank you:

Nick Grayston

Sir Stephen Tindall

David Benaym

Dame Joan Withers

Professor Akshay Mangla

Mark Lancellot

Rachael de Renzy

Elizabeth Joseph

Helen Saward

Igor Botelho Bernades

The Honorary James Shaw

Terry Tamminen

And my Oxford Said Business School J24 Executive MBA classmates for their worldclass support and friendship during the writing of this book.